Vicious

True Stories By Teens About Bullying

Edited By Hope Vanderberg Of Youth Communication

16

EasyRead Large

RHYW

Copyright Page from the Original Book

Library of Congress Cataloging-in-Publication Data
Vicious : true stories by teens about bullying / edited by Hope Vanderberg.
      p. cm. — (Real teen voices)
     ISBN 978-1-57542-413-2 — ISBN 1-57542-413-4 1. Bullying—Case studies.
2. Aggressiveness in adolescence—Case studies. 3. Interpersonal conflict in adolescence—Case studies. 4. Self-esteem in adolescence—Case studies.
I. Vanderberg, Hope, 1972–
    BF637.B85V53 2012
    302.34'3—dc23

                           2012015908

eBook ISBN: 978-1-57542-655-6

Photo credits from Dreamstime.com: cover © Fotoruhrgebiet, p. 5 © Archangel72, p. 12 © Draghicich, p. 20 © Alvera, p. 27 © Klikk, p. 33 © Archangel72, p. 42 © Liaj, p. 49 © Igorigorevich, p. 57 © Poco_bw, p. 64 © Jfeinstein, p. 72 © Adisa, p. 81 © Crisp, p. 86 © Marysmn, p. 92 © Iofoto, p. 100 © Marc Turcan, p. 106 © Conquista82, p. 115 © Imabase, p. 121 © Adambooth, p. 133 © Jazzid, p. 143 © Berlinfoto, p. 151 © Alptraum, p. 157 © Tracy Hebden

Reading Level Grades 9 & up; Interest Level Ages 13 & up;
Fountas & Pinnell Guided Reading Level Z+

Cover and interior design by Tasha Kenyon

10 9 8 7 6 5 4 3 2
Printed in the United States of America
S18860313

Free Spirit Publishing Inc.
Minneapolis, MN
(612) 338-2068
help4kids@freespirit.com
www.freespirit.com

TABLE OF CONTENTS

INTRODUCTION

Whether it takes the form of physical violence or verbal or online harassment, bullying can have serious and lasting effects. In this book, teens write about these effects from the perspectives of the person bullying, the bystander who witnesses the bullying, and the person who's the target.

Teens who are bullied often bear the burden on their own and end up feeling isolated and depressed. In "Feeling Different," author Isiah Van Brackle shuts himself off from his peers as a form of self-defense. The anonymous author of "Fortress of Solitude" retreats from her family after enduring years of teasing. It's only when these authors finally reach out to someone that they begin to heal.

Destiny Smith, who witnesses her friend become the target of cyberbullying in "'Smut Page' Survivor," learns that even when you're not directly involved, bullying can leave a lasting impression. As Destiny watches her friend try to recover her self-esteem and trust in others, Destiny realizes the impact of the Internet's influence when used irresponsibly.

Some teens react to bullying by becoming aggressive themselves. In "I Showed My Enemies—And Hurt My Friends, Too," author Elie Elius becomes combative to protect himself from bullying. It works, but he ends up alienating himself from his friends as well as his tormenters. And in "The Walking Flame," Eric Green begins to push people away—sometimes literally—to stay safe from bullies. But now as a young adult, he sometimes finds himself overreacting to the people he cares about.

Others take this line of defense a step further, becoming bullies themselves. "Since people didn't like me, I thought I might as well give them a reason," writes the anonymous author of "Bad Boy Gets a Conscience." He starts to bully others after getting picked on as a child. When he decides to give himself a personality makeover, he has to learn how to let down his guard and connect with his peers for the first time.

In "Vicious Cycles," Miguel Ayala also writes about picking on his peers after he is tormented nearly everywhere he goes—at home, at school, and in his group home. His interview with therapist Jonathan Cohen sheds some light on why targets of bullying often become bullies themselves.

"No one likes to feel helpless," says Cohen. Bullying someone can make a teen who has been abused or bullied feel powerful for a brief moment.

Cohen also warns that adults often underestimate how harmful bullying is. The target, the person bullying, and bystanders are all at risk for depression, and bullying can lead to more violent behavior. In the last story in the book, "How Adults Can Help," Miguel passes on some of Cohen's tips for how adults can intervene and help stop bullying.

In the meantime, teens can take comfort in the words of some young writers who have experienced bullying firsthand. In their stories, targets of bullying show not only how damaging this often-overlooked form of violence can be, but also the steps they took to get help and feel better. And writers who have been the bullies or the bystanders reveal themselves in a way that will give readers a better understanding of this pattern of violence that harms target, perpetrator, and witnesses alike.

The stories in this book offer a window into many teens' lives. You are sure to find within its pages people and experiences you can identify with and relate to. You might find that you can get more out of the book by applying what the writers have learned to your own life. The teens who wrote these stories did so because they hope that telling their stories will help readers who are facing similar challenges. They want you to know that you are not alone, and that taking specific steps can help you manage or overcome very difficult situations. They've done their best to be clear about the actions that worked for them so you can see if they'll work for you.

Another way to use the book is to develop your writing skills. Each teen in this book wrote 5 to 10 drafts of his or her story before it was published. If you read the stories closely you'll see that the teens work to include a beginning, a middle, and an end, along with good scenes, description, dialogue, and anecdotes (little stories). To improve your writing, take a look at how these writers construct their stories. Try some of their techniques in your own writing.

If you'd like more information about the writing program at Youth Communication or want to read more teen essays, visit www.you thcomm.org.

WHY ARE GIRLS SO MEAN?

by Anonymous

Oh, did you see the hole in Katie's sweater? It was mad big!" This was said by one of the "friends" my classmate Katie thought she'd made several weeks earlier. As the cries of laughter poured out from the gym bleachers, Katie stood with her back to the six girls, ignoring them. It hadn't taken long for them to shove her out of the group after she'd caught an attitude with the group "leader."

> **When I found myself laughing, too, I stopped and realized I was being just as mean as they were.**

Truthfully, I didn't care that they were laughing at her, because she wasn't my friend and I thought the hole was big, too. But when I found myself laughing, too, I stopped and realized I was being just as mean as they were.

"Why do we girls treat each other so badly?" I wondered. We take advantage of each other, compare ourselves to each other, and put each other down. We can be the most petty and fake people on the planet.

I see this a lot in school. At lunch I usually hear at least one group of girls talking about another girl they're supposedly friends with. I feel annoyed when I hear things like, "Didn't she wear those jeans two days ago?" and "I don't know why all them boys be fiending for her 'cuz she not all that."

Luckily, my friends aren't like that. My friend Felicia always seems happy and tries to lift my spirits when I'm having a bad day. Michelle's one of the smartest and most honest people I know. And Brittany is kind and considerate. On the rare occasion that I have a problem with my friends, I feel comfortable talking to them about it because we've known each other so long. We can be completely honest with each other. We don't talk behind each other's backs, unless of course we're saying something like, "Her hair looks nice today."

We weren't always honest and true to each other, though. When we were freshmen three years ago, things were different between us.

Brittany always seemed to be the one who needed the most attention. When our friend Brenda was obviously having a private conversation with her boyfriend, Brittany would go up to them and start annoying them. And she always talked on and on about her family and people we didn't know, while my friends and I sat there saying "Uh huh" the whole time. Sometimes, I admit, I just ignored her.

One day we were all sitting together in Spanish, where we always chatted during class. After finishing one of her long, boring stories, Brittany left to go to the bathroom. Michelle, Felicia, and I looked at each other with relief.

"I was trying so hard to listen to her but she just kept talking on and on," Michelle said. "I wanted her to be quiet." We laughed.

"Yes, she's always talking about her cousin and what she did to her, when we don't even know her," I added. We kept talking about her until she returned from the bathroom. I knew it was wrong, but I felt relieved that someone else felt the same way I did.

After that, we started to feel comfortable saying anything about her. We began talking about her out of habit. A few days after that day in Spanish, Michelle, Felicia, and I were in the lunchroom together.

Felicia said, "I don't mean to talk about Brittany's hair, but do you see how it looks? She hardly has any hair coming through her ponytail." We all laughed, and Michelle used her hands to mimic how much hair came through Brittany's ponytail.

That's when I started feeling bad. Her hair was somehow more personal than whether her conversations were boring or not. It was something she couldn't control, so it felt especially mean to talk about it. I knew Brittany would never talk about me behind my back. She may be a little annoying sometimes, but she's a loyal friend. Suddenly I felt so awful I had to say something.

"You know, we shouldn't talk about Brittany like that, because she's supposed to be our friend," I said. I knew they'd feel the same if they really cared about Brittany.

"Yeah, that's not right. You know, we shouldn't do that anymore," Felicia said. The mood was automatically serious and I could tell by our frowns that we meant what we said. Since then, we've never said negative things about Brittany behind her back.

I'm glad I realized how much I cared about her. Otherwise, we'd probably still be talking about Brittany to this day, or we'd have booted her from our group the way Katie got booted by her friends, and started making fun of her more. I think girls just get into a habit of talking about other girls behind their backs and end up doing it without realizing.

> **Many girls talk about each other because they feel more powerful when they put others down. Girl-on-girl cruelty is a kind of bullying called "relational aggression." Girls are more likely than boys to bully without using their fists.**

But why do girls act so mean? I think many girls talk about each other because they feel more powerful when they put others down. I decided to do some research to learn more about the problem.

I found out that it's not just a teenager thing. A Brigham Young University study recently found that this kind of behavior starts long before high school—girls as young as 3 and 4 exclude others and use peer pressure to get what they want. And many girls don't stop talking about each other when they become adults. Even my mom and grandmother often talk on the phone about my aunts and cousins. They may not be as mean as teenage girls, but it's still harsh sometimes.

Psychologists say girl-on-girl cruelty is actually a kind of bullying called "relational aggression." Girls are more likely than boys to bully without using their fists. When girls bully each other, they "use psychological forms that are harder to detect and easier to deny, and they can do it with a smile," said Tim Field, coauthor of *Bullycide: Death at Playtime,* a book about bullying.

I wasn't surprised to read that. This kind of meanness does seem to be unique to girls. I rarely see boys talking about each other behind their backs. I think that's because boys get their problems out in the open more quickly and don't hold grudges against each other. For example, my boyfriend Michael and his best friend Corey weren't always friends. They met three years ago in the boys locker room. Michael thought Corey was talking about him.

"You talkin' about me?" Michael demanded. Before Corey could respond, Michael punched him. Corey stood there in shock, and everyone around them said, "He wasn't talking about you!"

Michael apologized. A few days later Corey and Michael started becoming friends and left the misunderstanding in the past. Today they're best friends. That never would've happened if they'd been girls. They'd probably just have talked about each other behind each other's back. Even if two girls did confront each other, I think they would've ended up being worst enemies, not best friends.

I still talk about other girls, but only to say positive things, like "Her outfit is nice." I figure if the only way I can be happy is by putting down other girls, then I'll never be able to face my own flaws. I'll just continue to cover them up by focusing on other girls. I don't want to fall deeper into my own insecurity and become a victim of my words. Being able to accept other girls' differences and faults makes me feel like a better, more open-minded person. And it frees me to spend more time working on myself.

I SHOWED MY ENEMIES—AND HURT MY FRIENDS, TOO

by Elie Elius

To the reader:

As you read this story, there will be certain stuff I did that you will not be so happy about. But if you had been in my shoes, you might have felt differently.

I am proud of the way I used to act toward my so-called friends, the ones who picked on me all the time. It was good for me to learn to stand up for myself. But what I am not proud of is the way I acted toward those who cared.

Like a turtle, I built a strong shell to protect myself from the insults. But those who cared were getting shell-shocked also. Only I didn't notice until they all started to leave.

When I came to America from Haiti, I was very shy and passive. I was in a new country, I was the new kid on the block, and I was desperate to be liked. The best way I could make friends, I thought, was to fit in with the crowd. I used to let my so-called friends walk all over me because I was afraid that if I spoke up, they wouldn't want to be seen with me.

They told me I was down and I could hang with them, but later on I found out they were using me as a big joke. Phrases like "You hear the way that n—talk!" or "He looks so ugly and retarded" were constantly being thrown at me at home and at school.

I did not know English well and people would make fun of the way I spoke. Their words would sizzle on my skin like butter hitting a hot skillet. Plus, back in the day, my head used to be bigger than my body and a person couldn't tell me from a brown toothpick. All of these flaws added up to laughter and jokes.

Just for the hell of it, one of my friends would say, "Your father left you 'cause he didn't want your ugly ass."

My father, the deadbeat, left my mother before I was born, so my so-called friend had no idea why my father flew out on us. Still, just hearing him say those words made me feel hurt and angry.

I felt the other kids' words strike my heart like a sharp, pointy spear. I felt like dirt under their shoes that they could just wipe off. And, from around the time I was 9 till I was about 12, it went on and on. But then I began to decide that enough was enough.

> **I did not know English well and people would make fun of the way I spoke. Their words would sizzle on my skin like butter hitting a hot skillet.**

No, I didn't wake up one morning and say, "Okay, no more." But slowly, as I got older, I decided that I was tired of coming home from school crying. I was sick of avoiding my cousins, who also made fun of me, and hiding out in the kitchen if they were in my living room.

Reader, what would you do if you were constantly being picked on?

When I talked to people I was close to, they would say, "Pay them jerks no mind. Keep your head up at all times." When I came home depressed, my mother would sometimes say, "People picked on me all the time. Just ignore their talk."

But I could not ignore it and I did not know how to keep my head up. If I wanted this foul treatment to stop I would either have to (a) run away, 'cause I knew my mother would not move just because I was getting picked on, or (b) change my attitude and start wiping people off of me. I chose option b.

Change is a hard path to cross in life. Sometimes it is for the better; sometimes it is for the worse. Who really knows? Maybe the person who is doing the morphing does not know himself.

The good point for me was that I let a lot of people know I was not going to take their crap. The bad point was that I lost a lot of good people by being all hard. Still, the first time I really stood up for myself took a lot of courage, and I'm glad I did it.

One day, this dumb kid in my school went up to the board when the teacher was not there and started drawing me as a stick figure with mean little details. One of my so-called friends found this so amusing he had to join in. Of course, the whole class was laughing and pointing at me, and I felt like a rag.

At first I just went up and asked them if they could stop making fun of me because I didn't like it. Then my friend began to mock me and the other kid pushed me. I went back to my seat but they were still up there laughing, and the other kids were pointing and laughing also. At that moment I couldn't take it.

I remembered my uncle saying that if you want to get through to people, you have to be aggressive. So I stood up, walked in front of the class, and erased my picture. Where on earth did that courage come from? I have no idea, but I'm glad it came.

"What's your problem, you a—?" the kid asked me.

I said, "@#%& you."

It was right there and then I got into my first fight. My friend punched me in my face and the other kid kept punching me in the stomach. Even though I lost, this incident began the whole "Don't mess with me" sitcom. After that, I began to be more and more aggressive.

I didn't change overnight. I just always had that new attitude in my mind and, as time flowed, I began to pick up a few bad habits here and there. After a while I became a foul-mouthed little brat, and phrases like "just like your dog-face mother" would roll off my tongue with fire.

I did not go around spitting venom at everyone, just on the fools who messed with me. And of course I wasn't all mouth. I had a little action also, and sometimes I'd get into fights.

Day by day, my demons began to go bye-bye. People stopped picking on me and I had this feeling that I had accomplished something big. Infamy became me. The problem was that in some ways, I began to act different with just about everybody—not just with my so-called friends, but with my real friends, too.

> **Any little thing someone did to me, even if it was just a friendly joke, would make me snap or get ready to fight. Lots of times when I probably didn't need to, I kept my distance and had my guard up.**

Any little thing someone did to me, even if it was just a friendly joke, would make me snap or get ready to fight. Lots of times when I probably didn't need to, I kept my distance and had my guard up.

Plus, if I was hurt, I wouldn't talk to my friends about what was going on. I'd cut them out or get into a fight. That's how I lost my friend Syretta (not her real name).

I remember her party like I remember my mother's name.

Syretta was one of my best and most trusted friends. She understood me and what

I was going through. I could really talk to her about my problems and feelings. I loved her like a sister.

But for her 13th birthday, she invited some friends to her house for her party and didn't invite me. Syretta and I never had any beef that I knew about, so I was upset but I felt too embarrassed to go up to her and ask her what was going on.

So on the night of the party, I went uninvited. When I saw my friend Rafael, I went over to talk to him about Syretta. I was not as close with Rafael as I was with Syretta. We just played sports and chilled. But he was another person I could trust.

"You know that fat b—did not invite me. What she got with me anyway?" I said.

I guess someone might have overheard what I said because a couple of minutes later Syretta's mother came in my face.

"I would really appreciate it if you would leave my home. I do not like or allow this kind of rudeness in my house," she said.

I was so outraged that I actually went up to Rafael and punched him because I thought he was the one who told Syretta what I'd said. When I did this, everyone stopped and looked at me with disgust. Syretta's father called my mother. Then he dragged me out of his house.

At the time I was just angry. But now I feel ashamed. I was cursing and carrying on like I had no type of home training. And I feel bad, because even though I still don't understand why Syretta didn't invite me to her party, she really had been a good friend and I messed up our friendship.

I see Rafael sometimes, but it is just a hi-bye thing. And as for Syretta, I have not heard from her since that dreadful party. When I look back at the way I acted, I won't apologize for everything I did. It's important to stand up for yourself. In this world, if you want the honey, you have to kill a few bees.

Still, sometimes I kind of regret the way I carried myself. All that big and bad stuff wasn't me. I never wanted to go around attacking people like a pit bull. Times change and so do people. All that be-my-friend and I-don't-like-you crap is for elementary school, and that is where I left it.

When I went into high school, I decided I had to act and carry myself differently. I decided that when I entered the school building, I entered for an education, not to be liked, because looking for friends is what got me into this garbage in the first place.

At first I stuck by myself. But soon I found that people were coming up to me and wanting to be my friend, probably because I was just being myself.

I'm not a punk, so if fighting is the only way to solve a problem, okay. But I don't go to extremes, and I don't let that tough way be the only way I deal with my problems anymore.

Now if I have a problem or conflict, most often I will try to talk things through. Plus, now I know who my real friends are. They are the ones giving me something that I gave but did not receive before: respect.

USERNAME: HATER

by Kiara Ventura

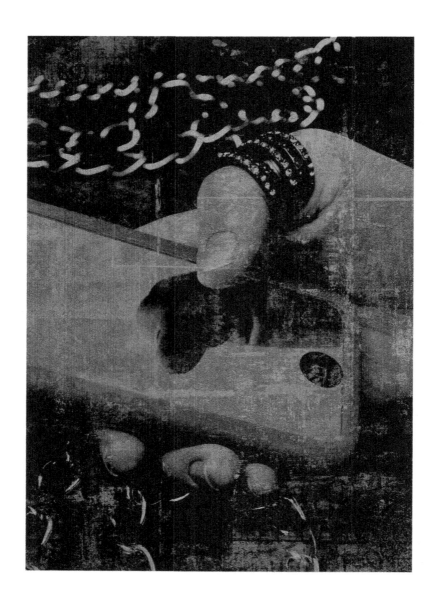

An unidentified person terrified my friends and me. Her words were anonymous and cruel, and she even made us worry for our lives. This person was a cyberbully.

My friends and I wanted to end the eighth grade in style. We didn't want to be just the nerdy girls in the honors class—we wanted to be stars. So my friends Mosammat and Thini decided we should perform in the talent show. It was a way to achieve school fame, and an adventure we could go through together.

> **An unidentified person terrified my friends and me. Her words were anonymous and cruel, and she even made us worry for our lives. This person was a cyberbully.**

We recruited a few more friends—there were seven of us in total—to perform an Indian dance, and began preparing four months before the big day. Mosammat and Thini knew most of the steps and taught them to the rest of us during lunch and after school. We would always laugh and joke during practice, and the stage soon felt like home.

Every day, we caught people peeking in the auditorium windows, looking interested. Soon, news of our plans started buzzing in the hallways, and we began to get positive feedback. We felt so supported; our dream of being known as performers was already starting to come true. But then trouble started.

"I'M GOING TO HURT YOU"

An unidentified person, whose username was "hoehoehoe91," began IMing my friend Frances, saying threatening things like, "I'm going to hurt you with a knife." Every time this person threatened Frances, she would tell all of us about it during lunch.

Soon, the threats were coming at all the girls in our dance group, as well as other girls in our class. She (I've always assumed it was a she, because the boys barely knew any of our business and seemed unlikely to get involved) would curse at us and call us names. For those of us in the talent show, it was clear that she wanted to wreck our performance and our self-esteem. She even threatened to attack us after the show.

As this was happening, we never used the word "cyberbullying." I'm not even sure you could call it bullying, since it was one person instigating something against a whole group. Maybe it was more like cyberdrama. But whatever it was, it wasn't fun. Some girls were straight up terrified. Others just brushed it off, assuming nothing would really happen. I felt like this person was just jealous, and I tried to ignore her.

The first time the mystery person contacted me, it was mid-February. I was on my laptop, chatting with friends on AIM, when I got a message from hoehoehoe91. She kept going on about how the talent show was going to be a disaster for us. I simply said, "Stop being so jealous. I am going to block you now." Then I took the mouse and clicked "Block hoehoehoe91." Her nasty comments didn't really bother me, but they did affect the focus of our dance group and cause suspicion in our class, since everyone was wondering who this person was.

> **It was a little creepy because she knew secrets about us, details about our relationships, and things from way back in sixth grade, but we still couldn't figure out who she was.**

For months, she continued to message the other girls who hadn't blocked her. Some of them IMed back-and-forth with her and tried to tell her off. It was a little creepy because she knew secrets about us, details about our relationships, and things from way back in sixth grade, but we still couldn't figure out who she was. Eventually, one of our friends told his mom what was going on and the school got involved. One day over the announcements, my friends and I were called to the principal's office.

HELP FROM THE HIGHER-UPS

As I stepped into the office, I inhaled the smell of fresh coffee. My friends and I all sat at a round table with the principal and a counselor and gave each other apprehensive looks.

"We're here to address the cyberbullying incident," the counselor said. "Tell me what's been going on."

We told her how this mysterious person had been threatening our whole class and especially the people performing in the talent show.

"Why didn't you guys tell us earlier?" the counselor asked.

"We didn't think the situation would get this serious. Plus, cyberbullying is pretty typical these days," I said.

"Next time, tell someone. I would advise you not to reply to this unknown person, and if anything happens, contact me. You are a part of our school and it's our responsibility to make sure you are safe."

I felt a huge wave of relief as I walked out of the office, and my friends looked relieved, too. We felt safer knowing that we had the support of higher authorities.

The person continued to threaten us, saying, "Everything is going to go wrong on that stage" or even worse, "I'm going to jump you after the talent show." But we all froze the bully out.

We remained worried, but we knew that the show had to go on.

CURTAINS UP

After four months of practicing, it was time. Not only were we nervous about performing, we were worried about our safety after the show. Ours was the last act, and as other students performed, we had mini panic attacks backstage.

But once we stepped onto the stage with bare feet, wearing saris (traditional Indian clothing) and bells, I felt beautiful and ready to conquer the world. We felt the wind from the stage curtains flowing open, and began to dance. During the performance our saris twirled in the air; our ankle bracelets jingled; we traveled along the stage to the rhythm of the music. We held our heads high, with smiles on our faces. We had the steps memorized perfectly, and nothing went wrong.

As the dance ended, I looked at my family members, who filled the second row. They cheered wildly, and from the crowd we got more attention than we expected.

Backstage, my father appeared.

"Here you go, baby," he said as he handed me a bouquet of flowers and kissed me on the forehead. "I'm so proud of you!"

"Thank you, Daddy!" I said, grinning. I felt so special.

Despite all the excitement, we were still worried about the threats. My mom drove me home, while my friends had school aides walk them home. It was funny to think that the school had provided aides to basically act as bodyguards for us. Thankfully, none of us encountered any trouble and that was the end of the messaging, too.

BULLIES IN HIDING

I believe this person was a pure hater. She saw us working hard for the talent show, got jealous, and tried to distract us with threats. But we pushed our fears aside and gave our school a great show. In fact, we did so well that we got requests to perform at an elementary school, festivals, and a Sweet 16 party.

Even though we never found out who the mysterious cyberbully was, we did learn how to deal with her, thanks to our school. We saw that if we kept engaging her, it would continue. Blocking her kept her quiet. Having the school behind us also gave us confidence about performing. If the principal hadn't called us in to talk about the situation, we probably would have quit the talent show.

> **I believe this person was a pure hater. She saw us working hard for the talent show, got jealous, and tried to distract us with threats. But we pushed our fears aside and gave our school a great show.**

I think cyberbullying or cyberdrama occurs because people feel that their voice is more powerful online. They can say whatever they want anonymously, without worrying about consequences. They hide behind a screen and try to ruin your life.

But instant messaging and social networks are supposed to help people communicate, not bully one another. I think people should remember that, and if they have a problem with someone, deal with it like old-timers and talk to them face-to-face.

THE WALKING FLAME

by Eric Green

As a little kid, I was feisty, but I did not have to look for trouble. Trouble came looking for me.

I was in elementary school the first time I was bullied. I was doing my schoolwork when a student threw something at me. I looked back to see who threw it, then went back to doing my work. First warning. When the student did it again, I said to myself, "Oh, hell no!" I got up from my seat and shoved that student against the wall. I said, "You wanna mess with me?" Second warning. He stopped.

> **I was teased because I was smart and because of the way I looked. I was a geek. I was humiliated by the whole school.**

But the bullying never let up. When I moved from Long Island to the Bronx, I was teased because I was smart and because of the way I looked. I was a geek. Yes, I had on those tight pants, suspenders, a tight long-sleeved shirt, and big glasses. If you saw me then, you'd be like, "Eric, you look like Steve Urkel! You look like a nerd!" Well, based on how I looked, I was humiliated by the whole school. It was not pretty.

When I entered junior high, I thought the bullying would be over. Wrong! But that year I decided there was no way in hell I was going out like a sucker. I had to let these bullies know that I could fight back. I started kicking and pushing anyone who touched me.

I remember when a student who looked like a punk tried it with me. He pushed me against the wall. Then all of my strength rushed through my hands and I pushed him back with full force. He fell backward and slipped on a big puddle of milk that sent him flying across the lunchroom.

"See, that's what you get when you mess with me, sucker," I said. I thought he would quit it, but the principal had to break up the fight.

High school was only worse. My personality changed. Remember Dr. Jekyll and Mr. Hyde? Well, I was like that. I could not take one bit of harassment. I became the "walking flame," warning people not to mess with me. Anytime someone spoke to me I was ready to go off.

I got a little paranoid. I even began to feel as if the teachers were bullying me. "Oh, that's just great. Just dandy," I said to myself if a teacher asked something simple like, "Where's your homework?" The way I saw it, my teachers were just harassing me.

My art teacher once said, "You're just like an old man, so rigid!"

"Why did you call me rigid?" I said loudly. "I'm not like an old man. I don't like to do things I don't want to do. I am what I am, and you're gonna have to deal with it whether you like it or not!" I was furious.

"Calm down, Eric. Don't be so sensitive," the teacher said.

During high school, I was bullied more and more because I was gay. Students approached me with personal questions—sometimes out of curiosity, other times to humiliate me. Sometimes it felt like being bullied was all I would experience in life.

> **During high school, I was bullied more and more because I was gay. Sometimes it felt like being bullied was all I would experience in life.**

Finally, I switched to an alternative school where the other students and teachers were much more accepting of my sexuality and my ways. Even so, it's taken me years to stop feeling like I'm being constantly pushed around and harassed. I was even furious with my mother many times when I felt like she was bullying me.

When I look back on what I went through, I get very upset. I hate the feeling of powerlessness I have been carrying for a very long time. For years I felt as if I deserved to be bullied because as a child I had nothing. I wasn't taken care of by my parents, and I didn't get much attention from my family or my foster families. I believed bullies picked on me because they saw that I was somebody who could not defend himself and had no one in life to defend him.

I wonder what I would be like now if I hadn't been bullied. How would I be different if I didn't have to watch my back when I went to class or didn't have to worry about being picked on while I was trying to figure out my sexual orientation? How would I have grown if I'd had more friends and could've taken the chance to be more of myself?

I wish I did not have to be the walking flame, always pushing people away just to be safe. The habit I developed of constantly defending myself has definitely affected my friendships. Sometimes I see teasing as a form of bullying. My feelings get hurt all the time.

I sometimes don't realize that I'm overreacting because even constructive criticism rubs me the wrong way. Then people say, "I'm just trying to help!"

> **I wonder what I would be like now if I hadn't been bullied. How would I be different if I didn't have to watch my back when I went to class or didn't have to worry about being picked on while I was trying to figure out my sexual orientation? How would I have grown if I'd had more friends and could've taken the chance to be more of myself?**

I feel so confused. I can't tell anymore if I'm being too sensitive or my friends are being too insensitive. Either way, the past bullying causes a lot of problems between me and the people close to me. Day to day, I still worry that someone will start harassing me for no reason, and that the terrible feelings of my childhood will come back to me at any time.

But sometimes it's not my imagination. Even though I'm 23, I still get nasty comments, usually about my sexuality. They still have the power to make my self-esteem sink to the bottom and make me feel like I'm nothing. When people harass me on the street, I sometimes wonder, "If I fought back in the past, why is it hard for me to fight back now?"

But I am older and don't want to fight anymore. I've learned that fighting doesn't solve the problem. So I just try to keep walking, and I say to myself, "Eric, those bullies are not worth your time."

FORTRESS OF SOLITUDE

by Anonymous

One day in fifth grade, a boy came and sat next to me in the cafeteria during lunch. Before I could react, he took my pizza from me and threw it in my face for no apparent reason. I got up and chased him around the cafeteria, trying to ignore the cackling and hurtful remarks like "ugly girl" and "dummy" coming from the other kids. This wasn't the first time I'd had to defend myself against my classmates.

When I was in elementary school, I didn't really have friends because I was shy and quiet and I focused on being a proper student. Most of the other kids in my school disrespected teachers and misbehaved. Starting in second grade, my classmates took it upon themselves to bully, tease, and totally humiliate me.

Even though school was bad, I always had a place to cheer me up: home. At home, I felt safe and invincible, like an impenetrable fortress that could never be brought down. My parents and three sisters accepted me for who I was.

They would hit me and call me degrading names like stupid, crazy girl, and b—. I was always anxious because I thought that every kid in my school had it in for me. My acting like a scared animal around my classmates only caused them to torment me even more.

But if I told a teacher a kid had hit me, he or she would wait until after class to punish the kid, or wouldn't do anything at all. I began to feel as though I was on my own to defend myself. I thought of myself as a weak person because I felt it was my job to stop the bullying and I couldn't. I felt vulnerable and alone.

Luckily, even though school was bad, I always had a place to cheer me up: home. At home, I felt safe and invincible, like an impenetrable fortress that could never be brought down. My parents and three sisters accepted me for who I was.

But even so, I didn't tell my family what was happening, because I felt it was my job to watch my own back. If I was quiet and they asked what was wrong, I would just get anxious and say, "Nothing," even though I wanted to say how bad I was feeling inside.

As the bullying continued over the years, I grew more distant from my parents and sisters. I still talked to them, but only short talks about my day. Somehow, they knew that I was having some kind of trouble at school without me having to tell them. They told me not to be fazed by it and to ignore it. But it was already too late for that.

I could see they were worried about me and I felt guilty because I thought I was a burden to them. After school I began going straight to my room, isolating myself from the rest of the family. I didn't want them to know how bad things were at school. Unfortunately, it eventually managed to reach home.

In sixth grade, due to the constant bullying and my rapid decrease in self-esteem, my grades took a turn for the worse. My parents started to lecture me that I could do better than this. I wanted nothing more than to tell them why my grades had dropped and why I had become distant from them, but I thought they would just pass it off as a pitiful excuse and yell at me even more. I was convinced that nobody would understand what was happening to me, so I kept the problem to myself.

> **After a few months of thinking about suicide, I also knew I needed to share my feelings with someone. I'm still not sure why, but I was afraid if I talked to my parents, they would think I was exaggerating. So instead, I told my teacher that I needed to talk to her.**

Meanwhile, the stress of school and home was taking its toll on me. I felt like I was going to break at any second. I became suicidal. I felt that because I couldn't talk to anybody, I would end my own life. I thought that maybe my parents and sisters wouldn't care if I killed myself because I wasn't acting like my usual self anymore. I thought that everyone would be better off without me. I pictured myself with a knife aimed at my wrists or my throat. I was planning to do it when nobody was around to stop me.

But then I thought about how my suicide would impact my family. Deep down, I knew that my family really did care about me. After a few months of thinking about suicide, I also knew I needed to share my feelings with someone.

I'm still not sure why, but I was afraid if I talked to my parents, they would think I was exaggerating. So instead, I told my sixth-grade teacher that I needed to talk to her. I sat down nervously and she asked what was wrong.

"All the kids in school treat me as though I'm their play toy. They tease, hit, and make fun of me. It's been happening for years now," I said. After that, I told her that I couldn't take it anymore and I wanted to commit suicide. At this point, I was crying and I was nervous about her reaction.

Her eyes widened, her eyebrows and face were perked in a worried manner. She took me to the school counselor on the first floor. He told me to sit down and then my teacher left the room to give us privacy. I got scared and wanted to leave, but I knew that if I did, my feelings would stay bottled up like a sealed jar of pickles.

It was silent in the room except for the sound of kids playing outside at recess. Then the counselor broke the silence and said,

"Everything will be okay. Just tell me what you said. It won't leave this room. However, if it's something serious like you planning to hurt yourself or others, or if it's abuse at home, I'll have to get you help."

That's when I got really nervous because I thought that by help, he meant putting me in a straitjacket and hauling me off to the crazy house like they did on TV. But I needed to get my feelings out and in the open. So I told him the same thing that I'd told my teacher.

After that, he called my home and told my mother to come up to the school as soon as she could. In less than 10 minutes she was there, sitting across from me with a worried look on her face.

I stared at the floor for a long time, struggling with what I wanted to say to her. I'd been hiding these feelings for such a long time. I was scared that I was going to be sent off to a psychiatric facility for the rest of my life.

Finally, I said, "I feel like I can't talk to anybody about how I feel. I ... I feel like committing suicide. Maybe if I do, then my family wouldn't have to deal with me." Tears began to flow from my eyes and I was shaking. I waited for my mother to say something. It was the longest wait of my life.

Wiping tears from her eyes, she said, "Sweetheart, you should have told us how you were feeling. We could have helped you with your problems. You should never have kept those feelings inside for this long. They could cause damage to you. You know that you can always come to us when you need help. I don't understand why this was any different."

To me, this situation felt different because the problem was in school. If the problem had been at home, I would have asked for help. But somehow I felt that since I was the one getting bullied, it was my fault and I should deal with it.

Later that afternoon, my mom took me to the hospital for a psychiatric evaluation. To tell the truth, I wasn't scared to go to the hospital anymore. I was happy that I had gotten it off my chest.

At the hospital, a small woman with short hair and light skin sat down beside me and asked me why I felt suicidal. I told her about how I was always being bullied and teased in school, how I distanced myself from my family and bottled up my emotions. I felt that I wasn't good enough for my parents and that I would never exceed their expectations no matter how hard I tried. I felt insignificant and isolated from my own family and I didn't want to feel that way anymore.

> **To me, this situation felt different because the problem was in school. If the problem had been at home, I would**

have asked for help. But somehow I felt that since I was the one getting bullied, it was my fault and I should deal with it.

The doctor told me that she had some problems when she was young, too. She said that people made fun of her head because it was the shape of a coconut. But she ignored them and focused on her own goals and people eventually stopped bothering her. She told me that if I have a goal that I want to reach, then I should just focus on that. Her words made me feel like I wasn't alone anymore—there were people out there like me.

I started meeting with a therapist every other Thursday. The more I talked about my problems, the more I felt at ease with myself. My dad took me to my sessions, and afterward he would ask how they went or I would tell him about them myself. Day by day, I started opening up to my family and spending time with them like I used to do. I could tell that they were happy to see me regaining my confidence, because they often had a surprised smile on their faces.

I was determined to do better in school because I wanted to regain a part of me that I lost during the bullying. I was fueled by the thought that I'd prove the bullies wrong and set them straight after years of being humiliated. Therapy taught me some ways to face school with a new attitude. I learned to breathe deeply to calm my nerves and to tell myself something encouraging each day, like "Don't let them get to you" or "I can make it."

One day during school, one of my classmates kept calling me names and poking me in the side. I didn't say anything or get upset. Instead, I ignored him and kept doing my work. The teacher turned around and yelled at him, which made him stop. After that, the kids in my class didn't bother me as much as before. I felt happy knowing that the therapy seemed to be helping me stay calm when I was picked on.

But things really changed once I graduated from my elementary school after eighth grade. In high school I was able to start over fresh in a place where no one knew that I was a target. I found people who had a lot in common with me and began making some good friends. By the middle of ninth grade I was feeling so much better that I stopped going to therapy.

There are things that I still struggle with, like my anxiety. I still feel nervous most of the time about my grades, asking for help if I need it, and walking through crowded hallways in between classes.

At home, I'm sometimes still afraid to talk to my family, and when I feel like I want to be alone I hide out in my room for an hour or two listening to music, reading, or napping.

Then my family steps in and tries to get me to spend more time with them like I used to.

It makes me sad to know that my family misses the old me. I miss the old me, too. I miss the feeling of wanting to spend time with my family. I don't like feeling nervous, isolating myself in my room all the time, and watching dust bunnies roll on the floor. I miss the fun, outgoing, and carefree person that I used to be when I was little. I'm not sure how to get back to that person, but I'm trying.

FEELING DIFFERENT

by Isiah Van Brackle

It was a brisk day. The wind was blowing semi-dried leaves, signaling the death of summer vacation's freedom and the rebirth of the oppressions of school. In the schoolyard, the other fourth graders were talking with their friends.

I stood alone on the sidelines, praying no one would see me and I could finally have a normal year, even if that meant staying free of human contact.

Memories of the previous year were still fresh in my head: going hungry because my lunch was stolen, stinging pain, warm saliva sliding down my cheek, and the sickening feeling of helplessness.

Unfortunately, the school bully took that moment to interrupt my walk down memory lane so that he could reintroduce himself. "Man, there are too many girls in this school. I think something should be done about it, don't you?" he asked me with a deadly edge to his voice.

I remained silent, glancing around nervously for the help I knew wouldn't be coming.

"Yeah, too many girls like you in this school, and it's up to people like me to resolve it," he said, pulling back his hand and balling it into a tight fist.

RRIINNGG! "Yes!" I thought. "Saved by th–" My thoughts were cut short as his fist slammed into my stomach, knocking the air out of my lungs.

I've felt different for as long as I can remember, like something at the core of my humanity is missing, separating me from everyone else. Growing up, the feeling was always there, even around family members. Though they were never judgmental, I trusted them as much as everyone else—not at all.

Although I craved human connection like any other kid, I had no idea how to interact with people, so I stayed away from them. My mother says that when I was little, she'd ask me why I wasn't playing with the other kids at the park, and I'd respond, "Because I don't know if they're good or bad." But I've always felt that what separated me from everyone was much deeper than that.

When I reached elementary school, I didn't know what other children my age liked to do, or the popular terms and phrases they used. That led to me getting tormented by other kids, and I began to feel that I wasn't worth the time to understand or love.

When I reached elementary school, I didn't know what other children my age liked to do, or the popular terms and phrases they used. That led to me getting tormented by other kids, and I began to feel that I wasn't worth the time to understand or love.

It got to the point where the only time I interacted with other kids was when they hit me, spit on me, stole from me, or threw my books (and sometimes me) into garbage cans.

When I went on to junior high school, things improved slightly, but not enough. The only people I made friends with were a few older girls. Unlike most guys my age, they could talk about things besides sex and dating, like life and our futures.

But being friends with them just made matters worse. They'd defend me whenever they could, and then when they weren't around, my tormentors would return and say, "Your girlfriends aren't here to protect you," as they proceeded to make up for all the harassment they'd missed.

Finally, I decided I'd had enough. But instead of fighting back physically, I decided to protect myself by cutting myself off from my emotions.

> **Finally, I decided I'd had enough. But instead of fighting back physically, I decided to protect myself by cutting myself off from my emotions. Once I became indifferent, my tormentors discovered it wasn't fun to bully me anymore and they stopped. But I still felt alone.**

After that, whenever I did feel some spark of sadness or anger, it didn't matter to me anymore. Once I became indifferent, my tormentors discovered it wasn't fun to bully me anymore and they stopped. But I still felt alone.

I began to watch people from a distance, trying to figure out what exactly made me so different. I observed people much like a scientist would. I watched their mannerisms and how their actions differed depending on who was around. I noticed things like an involuntary twitch or smirk that revealed what action a person was about to take.

After a while, I found that by just being near a person I could pick up on their emotions and use them to predict how a situation would turn out. I learned what to do or not do, what to say or not say, so that I could avoid conflict.

Once this ability came naturally to me, I found I was able to fit in with the emo and goth cliques because of my cynical nature and somewhat creepy way of not showing emotion. Still, I didn't connect with people. The relationships were all superficial.

I also found that once I started spending more time around other people and taking in all their emotions, I lost myself. I found it hard to distinguish my own emotions from those of everyone around me, and I felt overwhelmed.

Then, during freshman year of high school, I met a girl named Jade. She'd also had a rough past and we soon became close friends.

Because I still appeared indifferent, Jade would often tease me to try to get me to react. I usually laughed at her attempts and told her it didn't bother me, until one day it did.

We were in the lunchroom and she started her usual routine: hitting, screaming, and throwing condiments at me. In doing so, she ruined my favorite shirt. I don't know why, but something snapped in me. She'd finally managed to hurt me inside. I didn't say anything, but the pain was clear on my normally impassive face. She looked upset and didn't speak to me the rest of that day.

The next morning, I awoke to the sounds of thunder and walked to the bus stop in the pouring rain. The bus—when it finally came—wasn't much of a haven. Water seeped through the spaces between the windows, soaking me almost as much as the rain outside.

Two stops later, Jade got on the bus with a solemn look on her face—which was strange because she loved the rain—and sat next to me, as usual. She handed me a folded piece of paper and said, "There's no need to reply."

I unfolded it and found a letter of apology, the first apology I'd ever received.

I've found that writing poetry is the only way to truly express myself without any barriers. I compare myself to the moon because it's separate from the

> **world, floating in a void of nothingness. And while the moon may sometimes seem insignificant, it has the power to affect the nature of the world.**

For the first time in four years I had shown emotion, and for the first time I'd gotten a response, showing me how much someone cared. Since then we've been closer than ever.

Jade also unwittingly gave me a way to filter out all the overwhelming emotions and seal them within paper: poetry. Jade writes poetry to convey her pain, and she soon introduced me to the art.

I've found that writing poetry is the only way to truly express myself without any barriers. The moon is a focal point in many of my poems. Whenever it's mentioned, I'm talking about myself. I compare myself to the moon because it's separate from the world, floating in a void of nothingness.

And while the moon may sometimes seem insignificant, it has the power to affect the nature of the world. That's the way I've always felt I was viewed—a child worth nothing, deemed emotionless, yet capable of so much more.

These days, I see myself in a sort of limbo—stable but fragile. I've made progress, and I do find comfort in my friend Jade and in my family and the few people I now trust, and so for the most part I'm okay. But sometimes the feeling of being lost and alone gets overwhelming. No one truly understands me, not even Jade.

I want to finally be truly understood. I've always wanted someone who'd love me and accept me for who I am. I want a sanctuary, a haven for everything I've ever felt—someone to finally contain my emotions—and I want to be able to do the same for them.

"SMUT PAGE" SURVIVOR

by Destiny Smith

Names have been changed.

One day I was in school, on my way from math class to lunch, when I saw a group of students hovering quietly over something. Curious, I made my way to the front of the circle so that I could see what was fascinating everybody. As I got closer I realized that everyone was looking at Kendrick's Blackberry. Kendrick was a popular boy at my school, so I knew whatever he had his hands on had to be exciting. I moved in for a closer look.

When he passed the phone to me I realized that everyone had been staring at a Facebook page called "Smuts Who Burnin'." Once I saw the title, I knew what was going on. These "smut pages" got started back in the Myspace days when someone would make an anonymous page for bashing people so that others would come to hate those people, too. As we scrolled down the page, I saw pictures of different people the page creator had chosen to bash.

The people seemed to have been randomly chosen; they weren't all friends or people who had a connection with one another. A picture of a gay guy was posted first. He was in front of a mirror with a bikini on while his boyfriend hugged him. Under it, people had posted homophobic insults toward him and his boyfriend, "Peaches."

Another picture showed a girl wearing only panties. She seemed to have taken the picture herself, and it was clearly something she'd sent to someone privately, not expecting it to end up on a website where the whole world could see it. The comments belittled her for having a child in high school and for not being with her baby's father. One person posted that she was a whore.

There were a bunch of pictures like this, and under them all were rude comments from the page author as well as from other people. I felt uncomfortable looking at the pictures. There was no need for people to be saying these cruel things. They were taking it too far.

WHY DO THIS?

Then it got personal: I noticed a picture of one of my friends on the page. When I first realized it was Jessica, I couldn't believe it. In the photo, Jessica wasn't dressed provocatively; she was just sitting in a chair in her house, smiling. The author of the page had written that my friend was a dirty whore who had abortions for fun. Others degraded her by saying that she had sex with everyone in her neighborhood, and that she was broke and needed to get her life together.

I was baffled. I had known Jessica for years and these accusations about her were totally false. I couldn't understand

> **why someone would want to hurt her like that.**

I was baffled. I had known Jessica for years and these accusations about her were totally false. Jessica was a calm, friendly person, the type who would randomly start talking to you about anything, even if she didn't know you from a hole in the wall. She could start a party with the lights on, get everybody's fists pumping like they were in a techno club. I couldn't understand why someone would want to hurt her like that.

I felt Jessica had the right to know what was being said out there about her, so I called her at home later that day and revealed to her what I'd discovered on my way to lunch.

"Hey Jessica, can I talk to you for a minute?" I asked.

"Yeah, what is it?"

"Well, earlier I came across a Facebook page with you on it and people seemed to have some very strong opinions about you."

"What's that supposed to mean?" she asked, sounding exhausted.

"Well, it seems as if a mystery writer made a page bashing you and a few others, and it's gotten around."

Jessica didn't easily embarrass, so I figured she would just brush it off. Instead, she hung up on me. I called her back five minutes later.

When she picked up the phone I could hear her blowing her nose and sniffling.

"Are you okay?" I asked her, surprised to realize that she was crying.

"Am I okay? Is that a serious question? My picture is all over the Internet with people talking about how I'm a whore. Do you think I am okay?"

"I understand that, Jessica, but things happen. You're just going to have to get over it 'cause they already posted everything."

"Who would do such a thing to me? What did I ever do to deserve this?"

As Jessica started to ask me these questions, I started to wonder: What does anybody do to deserve that kind of thing being published for the whole Internet to read? Even before this happened, I'd always wondered why people would bother to make those smut pages. I always found them to be immature and showing a lack of self-control.

What does anybody do to deserve that kind of thing being published for the whole Internet to read? Even before this happened, I'd always wondered why people would bother to make those smut pages.

But it wasn't until I heard Jessica's reaction that I realized that cyberbullying is indeed a serious matter. On Facebook, you can upload the picture in different albums, write a description about the picture, and receive "likes" and comments on the picture. That's a lot of different ways to bash other people in front of a large audience.

"I FEEL NASTY"

For the first couple of days after I told her about the page, Jessica did not show up to school. When she did come back, she was not herself. Instead of wearing skirts and button-down shirts with her makeup done, she'd wear a black sweater zipped to the top with the hood over her face. Sullen and withdrawn, she secluded herself from our group of friends, not even sitting with us at lunch but instead going to the library or sitting alone by the window, reading a book.

I asked Jessica why she was staying away from us. She said she felt nasty. Everywhere she went, she felt like everybody was talking about her or looking at her funny.

At first I thought that maybe she was exaggerating, but then I walked her to her class. Sure enough, it seemed like everywhere I turned, somebody was looking at Jessica, whispering or shaking his or her head.

A HUG AND A SMILE

Then Jessica stopped coming to school. After a week, I decided to visit her at home. She answered the door in an oversize shirt, sweatpants, and hair that looked like it hadn't been combed in days. I just looked at her and gave her a hug. My once friendly, outgoing friend had turned into a quiet hermit.

It turned out that there was more to her reaction than I knew. Jessica confided in me that she'd been sexually abused when she was younger. She hadn't told many people about it. Unfortunately, the "smuts page" made the whole experience resurface, which added to her trauma.

I immediately assured her that the page was old news and that everybody had moved on to other things that week. She was not convinced, but after some persuading, she promised that she would return to school the following Monday.

When she returned to school she had on that same black sweater zipped to the top with the hood up around her face—not a good sign. I approached her with a smile to let her know that she was not going to endure the bashing by herself. For the next couple of days I walked her to all her classes and sat with her at lunch to get her back into the habit of being a productive student.

I approached her with a smile to let her know that she was not going to endure the bashing by herself. For the next couple of days I walked her to all her classes and sat with her at lunch to get her back into the habit of being a productive student.

THINK BEFORE YOU POST

Jessica has fewer friends now, because she's paranoid that everybody around her is judging her. I'm glad that she decided to return to school, but she's never been the same since this happened.

Jessica never chose to be the talk of the school. Going through this with my friend made me not want to go online anymore, since the Internet was not the safe place I'd thought it was. I found myself logging on to Facebook less and less.

If people would think about the effects of what they write before they post, maybe things would not get so reckless and out of hand. Everyone has the right to freedom of speech, but you still have to be responsible and compassionate toward others.

LEARNING TO LOVE MY HAIR

by Charlene George

A few weeks after I was put in foster care, my foster mother told me I was going to get my hair cut. I was 7 years old, and I couldn't remember ever getting my hair cut before. I had no image of what it would look like.

We went into a Spanish hair salon, and I saw lots of happy people coming out. I was sitting there saying to myself, "I hope I am going to be one of those happy people." But when I saw people's hair falling to the floor, my chin dropped. I was scared.

"Come on baby, you're next," said the stylist. He turned me to where I could not see the mirror. I could hear the scissors slapping toward my hair and I saw so much hair falling out. I was worried, asking, "Why do you have to cut so much hair?"

My foster mother told me to sit and be quiet. The man said, "Trust me, it's going to look nice."

When he finished, he turned my chair around and I looked in the mirror. I wanted to cry but I didn't want my foster mother to yell at me. It was too short—it only came halfway down my forehead. I was not very pleased, knowing it was too late now to take back my okay.

The other people waiting to get their hair done told me it looked nice. But I wasn't sure. I felt like a different person. The main thing on my mind was how all the people at school would react.

The next morning, I couldn't wait to get to school to see what everyone would think. I did my best with my hair and got on the bus. But then I started to feel nervous. I worried that the kids at my school were not going to like it.

A lot of people noticed my haircut, and one teacher told me how nice my hair looked. Then it happened. There was this group of kids who thought they were so cool. They always had something bad to say about others to put them down. They'd say things like, "Look at that fat girl," or they'd make fun of someone for not having on some brand-name clothes or sneakers.

> **As soon as they saw my new haircut they started laughing and saying mean things. I was so hurt. They had a lot of jokes for me, laughing and pointing their fingers. I thought it was going to stop there, but it didn't.**

As soon as they saw my new haircut they started laughing and saying mean things. I was so hurt. They had a lot of jokes for me, laughing and pointing their fingers.

I thought it was going to stop there, but it didn't. I hated having people judge me by my hair. They pointed at my head and called me bald, and even made a song about it at lunch.

The song went something like: "You're a bald-headed chick-chick, you ain't got no hair in the back, gel up, weave up, your hair is messed up." It bothered me so much I would leave the lunchroom or my classroom and cry my heart out in the school bathroom.

Eventually, my hair started to grow out, but that didn't stop people from making fun of me. And whenever my foster mother decided I needed another haircut, I got one. I didn't have a choice.

I used to hate to feel myself break down when people were being negative about my hairstyle. It made me feel so down on myself that I started to believe I was ugly, that no one cared, and that the world was against me. I felt like a piece of bread that a whole lot of birds were trying to feed off of.

I knew that the kids at school were not going to stop joking on me, so I had to plan something for myself to stop feeling the way I did.

For a while, I would try to fight back. I would make fun of how the other kids looked, too, like how one of the guys had birthmarks all over his head that looked like ringworm. I also did things like throw spitballs, curse people out, or just fight.

I decided that I was not going to let the other kids provoke me into getting

> **in trouble. I was going to choose the words that came out of my mouth wisely. I had to grow up and stop letting the things people said about me get to me.**

Doing things like that made me feel better, but then I would get sent to the time-out room or get suspended for a few days. I was going to start failing my classes if I didn't change my act.

One day I asked myself, "Am I really ugly like they say?" My answer was no. I hadn't been ugly when my hair was long, so why should I be ugly now?

> **If I had a card for every day I was laughed at, I'd have a full deck, but I decided I was just going to have to let them play out.**

I decided that I was not going to let the other kids provoke me into getting in trouble. I was going to choose the words that came out of my mouth wisely. I had to grow up and stop letting the things people said about me get to me.

Of course, that was easier said than done. It took me years to build up my confidence. But by the time I was around 16, I was ready to make some changes with my hair.

I knew I was getting more mature, so I wanted to try new looks. And I just wanted to feel cool for once. I started dying my hair and tried all different colors: black, light brown and dark brown, hazelnut, or orange mixed with red. I also put things in my hair like braids. I even wore my hair short with wet-and-go curls at one point.

Sometimes other people liked my hair, and sometimes they didn't. But I was happy trying all those new hairstyles. And wearing my hair in ways that fit my body improved my self-esteem, even though I was still being bothered by other kids in school.

If I had a card for every day I was laughed at, I'd have a full deck, but I decided I was just going to have to let them play out. Sometimes I would still cry or I would tell them things like, "I'm still going to have a wonderful day," holding a smile when I said it. Telling myself I looked good and not ugly kept me feeling positive about myself, even when people made remarks.

Another thing that helped me was two staff members from the residential treatment center where I now lived: Ms. Epps and Ms. Elliot. I looked up to them and thought of them as my stepmothers. They loved my hairstyles. They'd tell me my styles went with my features and made me look like an African princess. Listening to all the positive things they had to say made me feel better.

> ## Responding to mean comments by saying good things, or nothing at all, makes me feel happy.

Now I'm 18, and when people bother me I try not to listen to them. I know that what's important is not what anyone else likes about me but what I like about myself. I've put in a lot of effort to feel comfortable with how I look.

Now I hold my head high and make sure my hair is looking fine. When people make comments I'll say something like, "God blessed me just like he will do for you, and have a blessed day."

They may look at me like I'm crazy and say they do not believe in God, but I just walk away and do not pay them any mind. Responding to mean comments by saying good things, or nothing at all, makes me feel happy.

These days I still change up my hairstyle a lot. I like making my own choices about how I look.

I sometimes go to the extreme, like when I cut off all my hair last summer, even shorter than when my foster mother took me when I was 7 years old. I didn't really want to go bald, but my hair was falling out because of the chemicals and hair dyes I had been using.

But I worked my bald haircut with confidence. I accessorized with a head scarf, and when people asked me why I had cut my hair, I would just explain it to them and they understood.

I spent a long time beating myself up and not liking my hair just because someone else did not like it. It makes me feel good now to let everyone know that I am going to wear my hair however I want. Other people may like it or not, but I won't change it for anyone but me.

GAY ON THE BLOCK

by Jeremiyah Spears

Because I'm 6'6" and hefty, people often think I should be a ballplayer of some sort. But once you get to know me, you'll know I'm no ballplayer.

In my old neighborhood, guys would always call me out of my house to play basketball, knowing that was not what I liked to do. When I missed a shot they would ridicule me and call me a f—.

It's true, I'm gay, and though I look like your ordinary clean-cut Polo boy, I act a little feminine. When I'm happy, I like to buy shoes. I also like to read romances and family-oriented books. My favorite book is *Mama* by Terry McMillan. It's about a divorced black woman with five kids who's having problems being accepted into society.

> **I would never do anything that boys did, such as sports, play-fighting, or singing to rap music. I could never understand why anyone would want to harass me for that. I used to think, "So what if I'm gay? So what if I'm different? Accept me or don't accept me at all, honey, because I'm just me."**

In fact, I've been different my whole life. I first realized I was homosexual at an early age. When I was around 5 or 6 years old, I would see boys and think, "How cute."

Besides, I was labeled as different by many people. I never liked to play ball or get sweaty. My favorite toy was Christmastime Barbie. When the boys used to try to roughhouse with me, I'd tell them to leave me alone. I would never do anything that boys did, such as sports, play-fighting, or singing to rap music.

I could never understand why anyone would want to harass me for that. I used to think, "So what if I'm gay? So what if I'm different? Accept me or don't accept me at all, honey, because I'm just me." I couldn't understand why the boys wanted to bother me and fight me when they didn't know a damn thing about me. But they did.

The boys in my neighborhood were rough-necked, ball-playing, weed-smoking boys who picked on people to prove their machismo to their friends. I think those boys did what they did because of their own insecurities, because they wanted to prove they were manly men. There were about 9 or 10 of them and they lived in or around my neighborhood. Wherever I went I always ran into them, and often they would torture me for being gay.

One Halloween night, I went alone to catch the bus to go to a party. I was wearing a pair of dark jeans and a matching jacket and a black sweater with my initials on it. My mother had spent a lot on the outfit. The jacket alone cost $132.

> **All of a sudden a partially opened bottle of urine hit me and got all over me. Some straight guys think doing something like that to a gay guy is kind of creative.**

While I was walking toward the bus, I saw a group of boys on bikes passing by. I recognized some of the guys. The first thought I had was, "Oh no, they're going to start trouble with me." I kept walking.

All of a sudden a partially opened bottle of urine hit me and got all over me. Some straight guys think doing something like that to a gay guy is kind of creative. They all hurried away and I screamed and cried because of all the money my mom had spent on the outfit.

> **I felt the same as always—puzzled as to why I had to be their target. I thought these guys would never understand me. They wanted to change me. They wanted to make me someone I wasn't. I felt like the things the boys said and did were marks for life.**

Then I felt the same as always—puzzled as to why I had to be their target. I thought these guys would never understand me. They wanted to change me. They wanted to make me someone I wasn't. I felt like the things the boys said and did were marks for life.

For three weeks after Halloween, I had the incident on my mind. At first my brothers were trying to get me to let them beat up the boys. But I didn't think it would make the situation better. It would probably just wild up the problem more.

Finally I decided to show them I wouldn't stand for it anymore and I began to fight—with my pen. I wrote them gruesome letters smeared with ketchup for fake blood to let them know I was going to get them back and that I'd get the last laugh. Ha!

Usually, when the guys harassed me, I told them, "Go straight to hell because I'm going to be me and there will be no changes until I feel that my life needs a change." And I got revenge. I made fun of them for trying to talk to girls and getting turned down. Then I got physical with them because they tried to run my life, as if they were in my shoes living my life.

When we fought, often my brothers or my girlfriends would be there to help me—some of my girlfriends were known for beating guys down. And once I even whacked a guy with a plank. While I was fighting, I'd think about blood and more blood because of the traumatic experiences I'd been through. I wanted so much revenge on the boys who created trouble for me. Because of the fights, the cops were always at my house.

> **Even though it made me feel better for a short while to get revenge, I felt as if I was never going to succeed in having peace of mind. And after the fights were all over, I wouldn't feel much better.**

Even though it made me feel better for a short while to get revenge, I felt as if I was never going to succeed in having peace of mind. And after the fights were all over, I wouldn't feel much better. Often I felt as if I never belonged, and that no one would ever socialize with me because I was gay. I thought the world was so against me and that no one cared.

Still, looking back, there were people around who helped me and supported me, like my brothers and my friends. I can see how much of a difference they made, even when times were at their hardest.

When I was living in my old neighborhood, my best friend was Lauryne. We would go to the movies, the mall, or just hang in the park and talk about everything, from boys and love to clothes, shoes, and jewelry.

Like a lot of my other girlfriends, Lauryne didn't care that I was gay. As a matter of fact, she praised me for having the nerve to be able to come out at an early age to my parents and siblings and not really worry what they were going to think of me. She said things like, "You're brave," and that she was lucky to have a friend like me.

It made me feel wonderful to know I had friends who honestly cared about me. It made me strong and gave me courage to be even more open about my sexuality, and to encourage other kids to come into the light and take the risks. It made me believe there would always be people to support me.

Another person who really helped me survive everything was my grandma, who raised me. From my grandma I learned strength, courage, patience, love, heartfulness, and to treat all people the same no matter what. My grandma taught me to learn new things from people who try to reach out and teach you. She taught me the Golden Rule: Do unto others as you want others to do unto you.

My grandma was born in 1919. She grew up on a farm and was born during a time when blacks weren't accepted and women weren't allowed to vote. My grandma saw so much—the Great Depression, both World Wars, segregation, lynchings, civil rights. She would tell me about the marches, about the violence, and how once when she was in Jackson, Mississippi, she saw men cutting down two boys from a tree. She would tell me that life isn't that hard today, not after what she's seen and gone through.

She told me, "My dear, you haven't seen the harshness life can give you."

Sometimes people who have lived through hard times grow closed and mean and bigoted against people who are different from them. But my grandma had a strong sense of herself, and that made her open-minded to the different things in life. She always said, "People must know themselves before they try to learn from another person," and that's exactly what she did.

As for my grandmother trying to change me, like so many other people in the world wanted to, it never happened. Instead, she encouraged me to do what I thought was right and what would make me happy. My grandma often told me I would be different as time went on and that she'd always love me however I was.

Three months after I came into foster care, when I was no longer living with my grandma because she was ill, I received a call from my aunt saying my grandma wanted to speak to me. When she got on the phone, my grandma said, "I love you, dear, and don't let no one turn you around." Then she hung up the phone because she had gotten short-winded. Shortly after that conversation, she died. I loved her dearly and I miss her.

I now live in a group home for gay and transgendered boys. As for the boys in my old neighborhood, they no longer bother me, because I don't go around there very often. When I think back on things, sometimes I can laugh, but other times I'm still angry that those nobodies had so much control over my life.

> **When I think back on things, sometimes I can laugh, but other times I'm still angry that those nobodies had so much control over my life.**

Still, I think I have come to be okay being myself every day. Despite all the hassles I went through, the people who supported me made me feel that I didn't have to change myself for anyone. I know that my life would only get harder trying to change for other people's satisfaction. I know that I just need to satisfy myself.

A PLACE TO BELONG

by Lavell Pride

In 12th grade, I was at the prom, dancing with one of my female friends. She and I were grinding, winding, and touching on each other's skin. We were having so much fun.

"Look at those two, they're both gay," someone said. I turned and saw a group of guys laughing at us. They asked, "Why are they dancing so close, touching up on each other's bodies?" and "How come they're not dancing with guys?"

We didn't care what they said. But then a girl I didn't know called my name out, came over to where I was dancing, and said, "You homosexual b—." I ignored her, but she came closer and went on about how she did not like gays and did not like me. She said I was "fake" for saying that I was bisexual, since she'd overheard me talking about guys. That's when she yelled out, "I want to fight you," three times.

I told myself to relax and remember that I was just there to have fun. But as I walked away, she came behind me and grabbed my hair. Then I was so full of rage that I forgot the prom and we started to fight. Someone finally separated us and we cooled off. I saw her again later in the parking lot and approached her. I told her I was hurt that she was judging me unfairly and that I was being honest about being bisexual. And I told her I forgave her.

> **The sad thing is this is something I've become used to. I've been harassed, teased, and even threatened because I am bisexual—by kids at school and by strangers on the street.**

HURT AND ALONE

The sad thing is this is something I've become used to. I've been harassed, teased, and even threatened because I am bisexual—by kids at school and by strangers on the street.

> **People don't understand the impact of their actions. Just like every other teenager, I'm trying to figure out who I am. I try to shrug off people's jokes and harassment, but it still hurts and makes me feel alone.**

People don't understand the impact of their actions. Just like every other teenager, I'm trying to figure out who I am. I try to shrug off people's jokes and harassment, but it still hurts and makes me feel alone.

Despite other people's negativity, I've always loved who I am. By 7, I was already experimenting with what it felt like to be male by dressing up in boys' clothes and pretending I was a boy.

When I was 14, I started going to school dressing up in different ways on different days. Sometimes I would dress in baggy jeans and big T-shirts like a boy; other times I would dress like a girl, in tight jeans and dress shirts.

Acting and dressing like a boy, I felt more attracted to girls. I also preferred dressing like a boy in comfortable jeans and shirts. As a girl, I felt uncomfortable. Wearing skirts and dresses felt like I was trying to attract boys and show others, like my family, that I was a woman. It was like I had to show them I could be beautiful.

Some of my friends and other kids would ask why I would dress up in different ways and if I was gay or bi. I told my friends I was bi because I like to be with both males and females.

THE WAY YOU ARE IS "WRONG"

I felt happy with myself, but other people didn't feel that way. My aunt, who was my guardian, told me when I was 14 that being bisexual was wrong. I was just coming out of my shell in telling my family and friends who I was and how I felt about it. I didn't listen to her. I felt that I was doing something good for me, something that felt right from a very young age.

When I tried to explain this to my friends, they'd say, "Well, you're stupid and confused." I would get mad and try to fight them but sometimes I would stop because I knew if I fought I would be in trouble.

Other times I just wanted to cry. Ever since I'd gone into foster care, I'd felt alone. I wasn't getting love or support from my own family, including my three brothers and my father. I felt I'd missed out not having my mother around for help while I was growing up.

LET PEOPLE IN SLOWLY

Most of the time when I was feeling alone at school, I would go talk to my science teacher, Ms. Francis. I would tell her how I felt with the other students picking on me. She would just say I shouldn't let people get to me because if kids see that I don't like them picking on me they will continue doing it.

She also told me that I couldn't be telling everyone about my lifestyle, that I had to start by finding a close friend I truly trust and someone who I can see as a kind of family to me, someone I can share my feelings and my thoughts with.

> **I was in special ed and most of the kids didn't like me. I realized I was hanging out with negative people with**

no good thoughts in their minds. After talking to Ms. Francis, I saw that I had to choose what kind of friends would be right for me, people who wouldn't judge me for my sexuality.

She was right. I realized that I was trusting everyone with my personal business. I was looking for love, and trying to find support from those who did care. But I was being judged by the people I was telling my deepest secret to.

At the time I didn't have a lot of popularity. I was in special ed and most of the kids didn't like me. I realized I was hanging out with negative people with no good thoughts in their minds. After talking to Ms. Francis, I saw that I had to choose what kind of friends would be right for me, people who wouldn't judge me for my sexuality.

When I had some time to myself to think it over, I realized that there was only one person who was truly and deeply my best friend, and that was Jamell. He and I had been friends before we were in high school. Our friendship started at my family's church when I was 13 and Jamell was 12, so it was not so hard for me to figure out that he was my true friend.

I found out about an LGBTQ program. I thought it might help me find my true

> **self and let me know that being gay, bi, or les was cool.**

Jamell and I are like brother and sister. We look out and keep each other safe from people who try to hurt us and put us down. But I still wanted to be around other people who were just like me. I wanted to find a place where I felt like I belonged.

GIVING IT A TRY

After high school, I found out about an LGBTQ (Lesbian, Gay, Bisexual, Transgender, Queer or Questioning) program through one of my workers from my foster care agency. When she mentioned it, I thought it might help me find my true self and let me know that being gay, bi, or les was cool. I thought it would help me be more social and communicate more with other young adults so I could gain friends and trust more.

The first time I went to one of their meetings I was nervous. I was going to be in a group with people I didn't know, and I had to speak about myself.

But when I walked into the meeting room, I knew this place was for me. I saw some people sitting in a group in a circle all just laughing and having a great time. As I entered the center where the group was meeting, I saw drawings that had been made by teens and photos of trips and parties they'd had. It was so cool. I thought to myself, "This would be a great place for me to socialize, speak my mind about anything, and just have fun."

When I sat down I said, "Hi, my name is Lavell, and I'm 19 years old. I came here to see how this program works, to see if I can learn new things from it, and also gain friends I can trust."

After I introduced myself, everyone said, "Hi, Lavell," "It's nice to meet you," and "Nice to have you join our group today." They all looked at me and gave a smile. I told everyone what I was all about. I said that I was bisexual and that I didn't know if it was okay or if it was wrong to be having sex with two different genders.

At first I felt scared about telling the people in the group these things. But I did it anyway because I felt that the teens here were all the same in their own way and they all had questions and things they wanted to know about. That thought helped me loosen up more as I listened to others' stories.

"GO WITH YOUR HEART"

During the group, the counselor asked me who I was most attracted to and why I felt that way. I said that I was attracted to females more because whenever I was with a female I felt so comfortable around her and with myself. After I spoke, everyone clapped and thanked me for sharing my deepest feelings.

The counselor asked everyone else what they thought about what I had said and if they had any advice for me. One person said that she was going through the same thing. She said she'd made a choice to be with people who made her feel good inside, and for her that was females. She said she felt passion when she was with them and she didn't want that feeling to go away by being with a guy she didn't really care for.

She said to me, "You should go with whatever your heart is feeling. I followed my feelings because otherwise I would have stayed confused and felt unhappy, stuck in a place I didn't really want to be." I was shocked by what she said, because I felt the same way.

I COULD BE HONEST HERE

After the group session, they gave me a tour of the center. There were several groups offered, like how to start your own business, arts and crafts, writing clubs, music classes, and dance classes, including African and hip-hop.

I also made a friend. We began talking and she told me how she felt the same as I did about being attracted to females more than to guys. I felt happy that I had come. It was a relief to find teens who had stories similar to mine. I felt that it was a great place for me, a place where I could make friends and have people around who I could call family. I started going regularly.

> **It was a relief to find teens who had stories similar to mine. I felt that it was a great place for me, a place where I could make friends and have people around who I could call family.**

Within this group, I can be honest about myself and still be accepted. As group members, we get to take a chance to speak our feelings about what people say to us and how it affects us. I don't have to worry about someone going around talking about me and making me feel down.

Now that I've found a supportive place that motivates me, I want to reach out to other LBGTQ people. I want to let them know they don't have to listen to what judgmental people say about them.

Joining groups like mine would help them get out the emotions they have locked up inside and gain friends who are going through similar problems. Our group can't change the world, and negative comments will still hurt. But finding a supportive place can give us the strength and courage to be who we were made to be and discover the things that make us feel good about ourselves.

STANDING MY GROUND

by Xavier Reyes

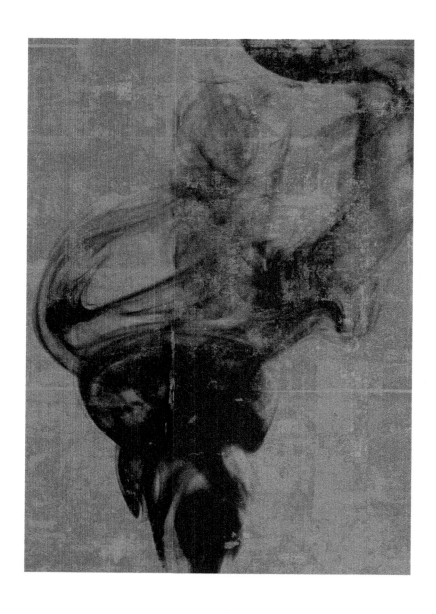

Yo Xavier, are you down for smoking some buddha tonight?"

"Chill, not tonight, I'm too tired."

"Fine, b—."

"I'll be a b—, at least I don't survive on weed alone."

"Shut up."

"Yeah, whatever, just get out of my room."

"Yo, don't ever say #!?@ to me again!"

"Trust me, I won't!"

Everybody in my group home was going to smoke weed that night. I was the only one who refused, but I didn't say no because I was tired. I refused because I was being pressured into doing something that I was trying to break away from.

Each time the word "no" came from my mouth, I was losing friends. But if my friends couldn't take no for an answer, then they weren't friends from the get-go. I was determined to stand my ground.

Each time the word "no" came from my mouth, I was losing friends. One by one they cursed me out and then left. But if my friends couldn't take no for an answer, then they weren't friends from the getgo. I was determined to stand my ground.

Soon I had nobody to turn to in the group home but staff. I would talk to them about the things that I used to talk about with my friends, such as work, girls, sex, and drugs. We'd talk about these things and they'd give me advice on how to deal with them.

When my peers noticed I was talking with the staff, they started to call me "teacher's pet" and stuff like that. Even though I didn't show it, this hurt me deep inside. The staff knew what the other kids were saying, but told me to ignore them because they weren't heading anywhere in life except for the men's shelter.

The kids tried to turn everyone in the house against me. They would say things about me to the new kids in the home, and I wanted to mess them up. But I knew that was exactly what they wanted, so there was only one thing I could do: ignore them.

The kids tried to turn everyone in the house against me. They would say things about me to the new kids in the home, and I wanted to mess them up. But I knew that was exactly what they wanted, so there was only one thing I could do: ignore them.

The other kids in the home began to steal things from me. They'd steal anything from personal hygiene stuff to underwear. One time everybody in the house ransacked my room. They stole bottles of cologne, clothes, jewelry, and more. The staff couldn't stop them, but they did help me get my stuff back.

After that incident, all the feelings that I had inside of me finally came to light—hatred, sadness, and anger. But I knew for a fact that I wasn't going to let these feelings take over my life and ruin it. No time soon was I about to give up. I was going to go out like a trooper, not like some damn wimp who couldn't control his feelings.

It took a year for my peers to realize they couldn't scare me into doing anything I didn't want to do. After they finally learned this, things changed between us. They respected me for who I was, and I respected them for who they were.

> **I learned to have confidence in myself and not put myself down because of the things other people say or do to me. If people can't respect my wishes and rights, then that's their problem, not mine.**

Today there are still kids in the house who can't stand me, but I don't care, because they aren't paying my bills or putting food in my stomach. So when they tell me they don't like me, I just tell them, "That's a personal problem," and walk away.

Nowadays things are much quieter for me in the group home. Once in a while the kids like to bother me, but it's only out of fun. The tension has eased up. Not everybody in the house is my friend, but I get along with everybody.

The main thing I learned out of this is to have confidence in myself and not put myself down because of the things other people say or do to me. I don't have to follow other people just to be down, and if people can't respect my wishes and rights, then that's their problem, not mine.

By not giving in to my peers, I gained self-esteem and self-respect. Bullying will always exist. Even though I seem to have defeated it, I know it isn't gone for good. It will continue to haunt me and you, and we have to keep fighting it.

THE FACEBOOK FIGHT THAT FRACTURED MY FACE

by Catherine Cosmo

Social networking sites are supposed to be a place for friends to connect and chat, right? That's what I thought until I was the target of aggression that spilled over from Facebook into real life.

One day, I was harmlessly joking around with a friend on Facebook. We were commenting back and forth on his status when all of a sudden, one of his friends—we'll call her Sara—rudely stuck her nose into our conversation.

For some reason I still don't know, she immediately began insulting me. For instance, she said that I shouldn't have been born because my father was too busy having sex with other men. She didn't even know me or my father; how could she make that kind of accusation?

I was angered by her senseless attacks. But instead of stooping to her level, I simply called her out: "I don't even know you. Why are you acting immature and insulting someone you don't know?!" I might've used the word "insane," but that was only to point out how irrational she was acting.

It was my first encounter with online aggression. I found it confusing. Why would this complete stranger come out of nowhere and, totally unprovoked, start insulting me?

It was no use trying to reason with her, so eventually I dropped it and walked away from the computer. When I later asked our mutual Facebook friend about Sara, he said she was crazy and always looking to start a fight. In the moment, I was disgusted and taken aback at how some people thrive off senseless drama.

It was my first encounter with online aggression. I wasn't blind to stories on the news about cyberbullying, but I'd never heard of anything like this happening to anyone I knew, and I found it confusing. Why would this complete stranger come out of nowhere and, totally unprovoked, start insulting me? It seemed she was doing it purely for her own entertainment. I guessed she enjoyed instigating conflict from the safe distance the Internet allows.

FROM VIRTUAL TO SURREAL

I was wrong about that last part. A couple of months later, I was at a friend's party. As I was about to leave, I saw a girl I recognized from her profile picture—it was Sara. She obviously recognized me too, because she lunged at me.

The situation felt surreal. What had been a virtual-world dispute was now landing at my feet, literally, in the physical world. I was shocked at what happened next.

Sara started wrestling with me, and I tried to keep her off me and prevent the situation from escalating. For two minutes we were going around the room in circles, holding each other's hair with death grips while she tried to kick and punch me.

Someone stepped between us. Sara was still pulling my hair, bending me at an angle toward her. Then I felt a blunt force against my eye and everything went white.

She released me, and I leaned against the wall to catch my breath. When I regained my vision, I noticed blood on my hand. I lifted up my head and saw a blurry room full of people waiting to see more violence. Clearly, this was like a dramatic reality show to them. One person was even videotaping it.

> **When I regained my vision, I noticed blood on my hand. I lifted up my head and saw a blurry room full of people waiting to see more violence. Clearly, this was like a dramatic reality show to them.**

Feeling immense pain, I hurried to the bathroom to look in the mirror. There was a gash on the corner of my eye next to my nose, and the whole right side of my face was already starting to swell and bruise. I could hear Sara in the other room boasting about her vicious kick to my face. When she saw me, she pointed and laughed.

Disgusted with everyone in that room, I left immediately. The next day, my mom decided it was best to go to the hospital since my face was badly bruised and swollen. It was a good thing we did, since X-rays showed I had four facial fractures and several scratches on my eye.

DOWNHILL SOCIETY

What happened to me points to one serious danger of cyberdrama. Yes, online bullying can be bad enough in itself, pushing people to depression and other psychological problems. But we should also be aware of the risk that a virtual confrontation will escalate into a real-life situation, maybe even a life-threatening one.

It seems as if interactions on the Internet bring out the most immature and vicious elements in people like Sara, who are probably prone to anger and violence in the first place. I believe that such people have been bullied or abused themselves and feel a need to make others share their pain. But by letting them hide behind a profile or a username while launching virtual attacks, the Internet may embolden them to lash out in physical ways, too. The Internet seems like an ideal place for bullying tendencies to intensify.

> **The Internet seems like an ideal place for bullying tendencies to intensify.**

Online communication can intensify other unpleasant tendencies, too. Humans have always had an instinct to look at violent acts, so I wasn't surprised when the 30 or so people at that party were glued to the fight between Sara and me. It did, however, sicken me that someone had the audacity to record it on a phone, and that the video found its way to Facebook, where many others would view it.

The world of reality TV shows has made people quick to view conflict as pure entertainment. When you combine that with the ability we now have to easily record things with our phones and post them for a large online audience, you have a giant step downhill for our society. The urge to turn everything into visual entertainment desensitizes people and makes them less likely to feel sympathy.

It also blinds them to the fact that when it happens in your own life, it's no longer entertaining. In fact, it is downright frightening and perilous, as I discovered when I was singled out and assaulted.

> **Humans have always had an instinct to look at violent acts, so I wasn't surprised when the 30 or so people at that party were glued to the fight**

between Sara and me. It did, however, sicken me that someone had the audacity to record it on a phone, and that the video found its way to Facebook, where many others would view it.

ALWAYS THE OUTCAST

by Christian Pimentel

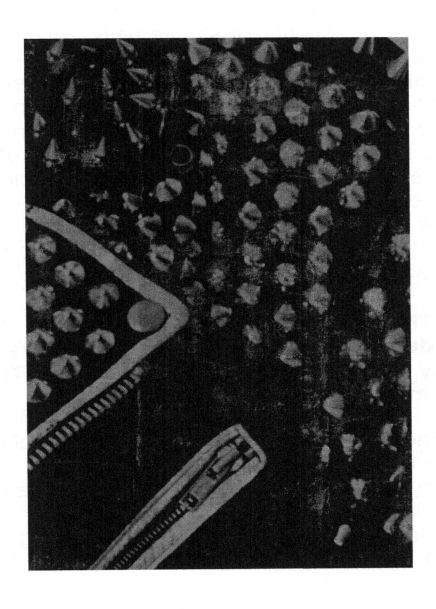

It wasn't even halfway through the first day of 10th grade and I was already in the bathroom wiping chocolate milk off my collared shirt. I had tears in my eyes, thinking of all the other times I spent my lunch hour cleaning cafeteria food off myself. I'd been bullied since elementary school—first verbally and then physically.

This time, all I had been doing was reading in the cafeteria when, out of nowhere, someone threw chocolate milk at me. It hit me hard and I felt frozen. Then someone sat in front of me with a tray of food. I thought he was going to talk to me or help me clean up, but instead he threw the tray at my face. As I got up, more kids threw food at me, along with plastic forks and paper balls.

The laughter just got louder and louder. I could taste the salty tears as they dripped down to my lips. They seemed like never ending tears.

The laughter just got louder and louder. I could taste the salty tears as they dripped down to my lips. They seemed like never ending tears.

I looked in the bathroom mirror, hating what I saw. After having all that stuff thrown at me and hearing people say I was ugly and that my clothes were geeky, I started to think it might be true. At that moment, I felt like no one wanted to be my friend, and I thought that this school year ahead was going to be the same as all the rest—awful.

LOOKING FOR FRIENDS

A couple of days later I saw a group of interesting-looking kids talking in the cafeteria. I hoped that if I could find my own group of friends, maybe I wouldn't be so lonely or get bullied anymore. Before, when I had tried to meet people, they would laugh and walk away. But I was feeling optimistic that day and said to myself, "I'm cool and nice and anyone would love to be my friend."

I saw a kid with a lip piercing, wearing all black. He looked like he had stepped out of a rock music video. One of his friends also had a lip piercing and a big green Mohawk, and they were with a few other kids with black clothes, piercings, and cool hairstyles. They seemed so different. I always felt different and I liked their style, so I thought that we might get along.

I went and sat with them and said hello. They ignored me, but I still thought they looked like the coolest people ever.

SHOPPING TO FIT IN

People with unique clothing had attracted me since I was little, but I hadn't thought of changing the way I dressed until now. I thought that if I looked like them, maybe they would accept me into their group. When I arrived home I asked my mother if we could go shopping.

We went to a couple commercial retail stores, where my mom picked out jeans, khakis, and button-down shirts. I looked at them in disgust. She always dressed me in simple, boring clothes that made me look like an old man going to church. But I didn't want to look boring because, after all, I didn't feel like I was a boring person.

We went to another store and I saw long, black skinny pants like the ones the Mohawk kid had worn. I thought I could wear them with cool black boots. I purchased the pants (even though my mother disliked them) and a pair of alternative-looking sneakers. I went home with my new clothes knowing I would fit in better with the pierced kids.

I went to school the next day wearing my new pants and shoes, along with a rocker shirt and black leather jacket I had gotten as gifts from my aunt. At lunch, I sat alone in the cafeteria hoping that those cool, different kids would notice me. When they ignored me, I felt so stupid for trying to fit in with them. I figured I should just accept being alone.

GETTING RID OF THE OLD ME

Although I didn't make any friends with my new clothes, I decided to keep the look. It felt good wearing something that stood out. I had always been different, even with conservative clothing on, and now how I looked finally matched my personality. I felt more comfortable and confident in my new clothes.

A couple of weeks later, I even put on some black eyeliner and black nail polish before school. When I came out of the bathroom, my mother saw me and ordered me to clean it off. I did, but when I got to school I went to the bathroom and put the eyeliner on again. I looked at myself and thought, "Where's my guitar?" The little boy who wore the button-down shirts and slacks, the boy who was teased and was always lonely, was gone. I looked like a different person and it felt good.

On my way to class the other kids looked at me weird, and I heard some of them criticizing me. I didn't care. I had heard it all before. Then one of the kids in all black with piercings said, in a low raspy voice, "You look so cool." His friends who were standing nearby agreed.

I looked at them more closely now than I had before, and thought they actually seemed like clones of each other. I ignored them and went to math class. But later in the day, they spoke to me again. This time, I was tired of being alone, so I finally started talking to them.

ALL FOR THEIR AMUSEMENT

Over the next few weeks, we talked more often. Then, one day after art club, one of the members of the group invited me to hang out. I was ecstatic. As we were leaving the school, he stopped to talk to one of his friends. I saw them laughing, but I couldn't hear what they were saying. When he came back I decided to ignore it, and we went to St. Mark's Place together.

As we headed out, he offered me a cigarette. I didn't want to take one because I have asthma, but I thought, "Why not?" We ended up smoking his whole pack and then shoplifted some cool merchandise that matched our look. I didn't have a big problem with smoking or shoplifting, though I knew I was doing it just to fit in.

I was disappointed, and mad at myself for trusting those kids. I felt like I should have known from the beginning that they would mistreat me.

As we walked around, we talked openly. For the next few days I hung with him and his friends. Sometimes we would all call each other and just spend a long time talking. I thought I finally had friends. I was elated.

Then, suddenly, it all changed. I realized they were spreading false information about me around the school. As a result, other kids started coming up to me saying vulgar things. People who never knew me even started to make fun of me because of the rumors. I realized the kids in black didn't actually like me; they were just using me for their amusement.

Their actions didn't surprise me that much since other kids had mistreated me for years. But I was disappointed, and mad at myself for trusting those kids. I felt like I should have known from the beginning that they would mistreat me.

After that, I decided I didn't need friends. What was the point when everyone was the same? I went back to reading alone in the cafeteria and having food thrown at me.

MY SYMBOLIC ARMOR

Looking back, I realized I had fallen into that group's trap because I was desperate to be part of something, to feel like I belonged somewhere. I thought the Mohawk and piercings meant that those kids were different from others, that they would be more open-minded and less judgmental. I thought that they would accept me unconditionally. But I was wrong. A few piercings don't automatically make you a better person.

> **I thought the Mohawk and piercings meant that those kids were different from others, that they would be more open-minded and less judgmental. I thought that they would accept me unconditionally. But I was wrong. A few piercings don't automatically make you a better person.**

At the same time, the good part about that terrible experience was that I began to feel more confident about expressing myself, and I found a look I am comfortable in. I had always wanted to look different, and now I do. Before, I had felt like a puppet; my mom chose my clothes for me and I let other kids control how I felt about myself. Now, I feel more powerful choosing my own clothes and just being myself.

I still get mistreated by kids who see me as an easy target, but it doesn't hurt me as much as it used to. My clothes symbolize protective armor I've put up against anyone trying to ridicule me. They say, "This is who I am and I don't care what you think about it."

Now, whenever someone calls me a name, I tell myself something positive to counteract it.

Of course, part of me still feels a longing to be in a place where I will be accepted by people who won't judge me, in a world where I don't need protective armor.

CAUGHT BETWEEN TWO COLORS

by Shaniqua Sockwell

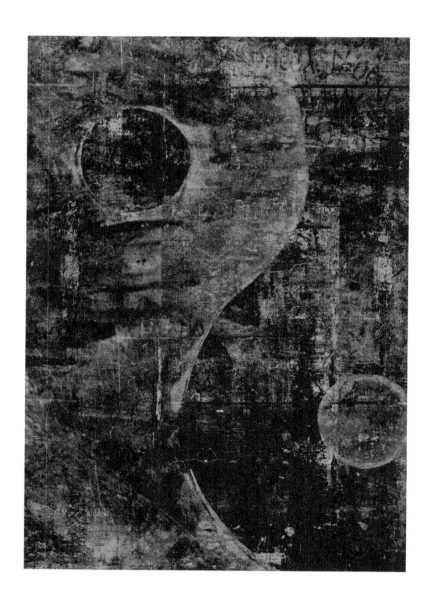

When I was a little girl growing up in the Bronx, I would sit on the front steps of my apartment building and watch people walk by. White people, Spanish people, Indian people, and, of course, black people. A world full of color, each person unique and special in her own way.

And I began to wonder: Why, with all this beauty in the world, must we hurt one another? Why can't we love our differences, rather than hate each other for them?

Which brings me to my story. If anyone knows anything about being hated for being different, it's me.

From the time I was 3, I was always told by friends, teachers, and even family that I was "different" from "everyone else." They didn't tell me exactly how I was different or who "everyone else" was, but when I was 7 years old I found out.

> **Why, with all this beauty in the world, must we hurt one another? Why can't we love our differences, rather than hate each other for them?**

A girl at school named Maxine would pick fights with me every day and do her best to get me yelled at. Whenever she got herself in trouble, she would find a way to blame me. I seemed to be the only person she ever picked on and she made my life miserable. She was, in a sense, my own personal bully.

One day after school, Maxine and her friends caught up with me while I was walking home. She tapped me on the shoulder and said, "Hey Shaniqua, what you get on the history test?"

"I got an 80. Why?" I asked.

She pinned me against a car and yelled, "Well, I only got a 65, b—! You should've let me see your test paper, but you had to be Ms. Goody Two-Shoes, didn't you?"

"Let go of me! At least you passed!" I said.

She pulled back her hand like she was ready to slap me, but instead she turned to her friends and said, "You ain't even worth it." Then she shoved me. "Bye, you wanna-be white b—!"

> **A girl at school named Maxine would pick fights with me every day. I seemed to be the only person she ever picked on and she made my life miserable. She was, in a sense, my own personal bully.**

I don't know why, but when she said that, something inside me clicked. As Maxine was walking away I said, "I'm not a wanna-be white b." (I was never comfortable cursing.)

She turned back around and started to laugh. Then she said, "Who you think you foolin'? You walk white, talk white, and you dress white, too. With all that preachin' you be doing at school about love and understandin',

I thought at least you'd act like your own people. But no, you gotta be Ms. Proper."

Maxine snickered. I glared at her and said, "I never said I was proper and I don't go around preaching anything."

"Do you listen to yourself?" she asked me. Her friends said they had to go, which left me alone with Maxine.

"Listen to you. Don't nobody in school talk like you 'cept the white kids. Instead of sayin', 'Yeah,' you say, 'Yes.' Instead of sayin', '#!?@ you,' you say, 'Forget you.' I don't know if you know it or not, but you is different with a capital D! If you ain't realized that yet, you's one blind b—!"

I didn't want to say that I'd been hearing I was different for a long time now (especially since the way Maxine said it made me think it was really true).

So instead I said, "Oh, so you're saying that I've got to dress in tight clothes, get bad grades, and talk with broken English in order to be normal."

"B—, I ain't sayin' #!?@ 'cept this. Before you start talkin' about black this and black that, find the black in you first. Bye b—, see ya tomorrow." Then she walked away.

So that's what everyone meant when they said I was "different." They thought I acted white and not black. "Is that a bad thing?" I wondered.

I thought about what Maxine said as I walked the rest of the way home, and I tried to convince myself that I was black. I kept on repeating to myself, "I am black, I am black." Wasn't I?

When I finally got home my brothers were watching TV, but when they saw me they jumped up and said, "Nica, we hungry."

I went over and gave them a kiss and said, "Daddy never came over to make dinner for you?"

"He in kitchen," Lewis said. "But he cook too slow."

"What about Mommy?" I said.

"She no come home," Lewis said. He had this sad, faraway look in his eyes. I hugged him and told him everything was going to be all right, although I wasn't so sure myself. I knew why she wasn't home, and, even though they were young, so did my brothers.

She was out getting high and it was no secret to us. I wish she knew what kind of pain she was putting us through. Maybe if she did know, she wouldn't have been out there shooting up and sniffing her life away.

I went in the kitchen and saw my father searching in the fridge. When he finally looked up and saw me, he said, "Hey girl, what's up."

"Nothing much," I said. "Could I talk to you for a sec?"

"Sure, honey. Just a sec." He looked in the fridge and sucked his teeth. "Looks like you'll be going to Grandma's house tonight to eat." Then he closed it. "Okay, what's up?"

"Well, there's this girl named Maxine in my school and she told me that I act white. People say that I act different, and I think that's what they mean. Do you think there's something wrong with me?"

"Sweetie, come here."

I sat down in the chair in front of him.

"Now, there's nothing wrong with you. You're a smart young lady for your age. There is nothing wrong with the way you act. Just because you don't talk or walk like everyone else, that's no reason to feel uptight about yourself. There is no one way to be, anyway. So if someone teases you about something, don't listen to them. Just believe in yourself."

"Thanks Daddy," I said, and hugged him.

After my little talk with Dad, I was no longer afraid to express myself, whether I "sounded white" (whatever that means) or not. I got over my fear of being "different" by believing in myself.

From that point on I avoided Maxine. Whenever she tried to start trouble with me, I would tell her to leave me alone.

We all bleed, cry, laugh, and die the same way. It doesn't matter what people say about you or what's on the outside.

> **It's what's on the inside and what you think about yourself that counts.**

If someone like Maxine ever happens to come along and harass you because they find you different, just tell her: "You can harass me if you want to and call me names, but no matter what you do, I'm gonna be who I am."

My message is this: Whether you are white and "act black" or are black and "act white," we all bleed, cry, laugh, and die the same way. It doesn't matter what people say about you or what's on the outside. It's what's on the inside and what you think about yourself that counts.

THE VERY LONELY BULLY

by Avad Ratliff

One day I went into my foster brother's room and saw all kinds of games and toys. So when he came in the room, I asked, "John, can I play with your games?"

"No, get out of my face—you're not a part of this family. And don't go through my stuff."

"I didn't go through your stuff," I said, grabbing him by the neck. "N—, I want to play with those games."

"Ouch, stop hitting me," he said. But everything I wanted, that's how I got it: "Gimme that, n—, I want it." In a lot of my foster homes, bullying seemed like the only way.

I was treated badly in my foster homes and missed my family. I didn't know how to deal with being alone. I felt bad so often that I became a bully.

Ever since I went into foster care when I was 6, I'd been feeling angry and alone. The Administration for Children's Services took me away from my home because my father hit my mother, my mother left home to protect herself, and my father became abusive and controlling toward us kids.

The day Children's Services came, I wanted to stay with my father because I was scared and I didn't know where I was going. The worker didn't even tell me where or why she was taking us. Then we got split up and all my brothers and sisters went their own way.

In my first foster home, I didn't see my family for a long time—about a year and a half. I felt abandoned, like I was just passed down to a family that didn't like me and treated me like a stranger. I didn't know how to express what I was feeling, so I really acted out. I snuck ice cream, made prank phone calls to the police, and acted wild.

> **I was treated badly in my foster homes and missed my family. I didn't know how to deal with being alone. I felt bad so often that I became a bully.**

I missed my brother, especially. All I could do was sit in the house and daydream about the good times I'd had with my brother. Thinking about him made me feel happy, but later I would miss him and feel sad. Then I didn't have anybody to comfort me. The foster family didn't seem to care if I cried or if I was mad. They only seemed to care if I damaged anything in their house.

Finally, I got to see my mother. I missed her so much that I didn't know how to act the day I saw her. I was running and bouncing off walls and buying out the candy store.

After that visit, I eventually went home for a couple of years. At home I felt a little calmer. I had friends who lived around my way, I played basketball, and I watched movies with my mother.

But in truth, being home didn't stop me from bullying kids at school or around my neighborhood. I still felt angry from being away from home for so long, and I was mad at my father for breaking up the family. I didn't care about anybody or their feelings, just mine and what I wanted.

And soon I went back into the system. This time, I went through a lot of different foster homes and group homes. I had to make new friends all over again, and I had a real hard time doing that.

I couldn't make friends because I would always take my anger out on them. I'd want to fight all the time. I lost most of my friends, and that made me feel really sad, because most of the time I didn't mean to make things get out of hand. That kept me feeling guilty for a long time.

I was even more of a bully in my foster home. If the foster mother made me do things I didn't want to do, like wash the dishes even though other kids were at home, too, I would get mad and take it out on the other foster kids.

> **I couldn't make friends because I would always take my anger out on them. I lost most of my friends, and that made me feel really sad. I didn't mean to make things get out of hand.**

I felt lonely inside. To keep from feeling attached to any of my foster parents, I stopped myself from trusting people. I shut everyone out of my life. When I didn't have anybody to talk to, it didn't feel good. I felt like I was the saddest person in the world.

Holding everything inside and not talking to anybody made my sadness turn to anger. I started to feel angry every time my family visited me because I didn't want them to leave. I wanted to go home with them. Visiting my family and then having to go back to the foster homes was even harder. Between those times I was not happy at all.

When I was 12, I ended up in a residential treatment center, and that's where I learned how to talk to someone and trust someone. That helped me get a lot of problems off my chest, which helped me stop getting mad and taking my anger out on my friends.

My mentor, Tammy, was 22 and lived in New Jersey. She came from a wealthy family, and she was never in foster care. But she was a good mentor to me for about five years.

We met on the campus football field one day when all the mentors came to play with us. We were all playing when a guy squeezed my damn ribs and I dropped the ball. We started fighting.

The staff tried to restrain me. My mentor came at the right moment. We sat down and talked about why I punched him and what happened. She calmed me down and from then on I liked her.

Tammy was nice. She took me out, helped me with schoolwork, and taught me a little bit of Chinese. Most of all she always listened to me and let me talk to her about my problems. She never tried to make me talk, she never tried to change me, and she never made it seem like my past was my fault. When I got in trouble, Tammy gave me the benefit of the doubt. That helped me trust her.

She also kept our conversations confidential. I feel that the only way you know if you can trust somebody is if you tell them a secret, so one time I told her that I missed my family and I was going to run away to my real home. She didn't tell any doctors or any social workers, she just talked to me and gave me a lot of advice and solutions to my problems.

> **Tammy was nice. She never tried to make me talk, she never tried to change me, and she never made it seem like my past was my fault. When I got in trouble, Tammy gave me the benefit of the doubt. That helped me trust her.**

From then on I trusted her, and I learned a lot from her. Every time Tammy came to the campus she took me out. We went to the movies a lot, and on Thanksgiving she took me to her mother's house in New Jersey where I got to meet her family.

Most of all, Tammy taught me how to calm down. If I got mad, she would hold me and let me explain what happened. Her hugs were what did it for me. I'd never had a hug when I was in the residential center.

Tammy also taught me how to be the bigger man. I was the type of person who thought, "If you want to fight, let's go." I didn't waste any time. If she saw me about to fight, she would say, "Put your hands down," and, "If he hits you, he's wrong and you're right." Then she would ask me. "Which one is better?" Before you know it, I grew out of fighting, because it started to seem childish to me. I started to see that what I was doing was wrong, like bullying and being disrespectful and selfish.

Tammy helped me get closer to my mother, too. She knew I missed my family and let me call my family when we hung out. Sometimes she took me to my house to let me see my mother.

My mother also proved that she was sticking with me. One time when I was in the residential center, I was getting bullied by the staff and some of the residents. My mother came there and shut all that down. That helped me a lot.

My mother is young and beautiful, with jet-black hair and pretty eyes (that's for those millionaires out there). She's sweet and giving.

She often sat me down and talked to me about how to act in school. She also told me, "Call me if you need anything."

> **My mother taught me that it wouldn't help me to blame her, myself, or anyone else for what I'd been through. Knowing that helped me get closer to people without blaming them for my problems.**

The best thing my mother did, though, was sit me down and explain to me why I'd been in foster care when I was little. She told me that after she left my father and we went into foster care, the system wouldn't let us go home to her unless she had an apartment and a job. That was hard, so it took a while.

I still felt upset that we spent so much of our lives apart, but I started to feel better because I finally knew it wasn't my fault and that it wasn't my mother's fault either.

Knowing that my mother fought like hell to get me out of foster care felt good. But my mother also told me that there are going to be times when she can't help me, like when I'm on the campus fighting and getting in trouble. My mother taught me that it wouldn't help me to blame her, myself, or anyone else for what I'd been through. Knowing that helped me get closer to people without blaming them for my problems.

With the help of my mentor and my mom, I started to be able to turn my life around a little bit. They taught me that when I throw away friendships, I have nobody to talk to. Then I hold my problems inside and just feel worse.

Once I started to taste how it felt to have friends, I didn't want to give them up. I had to learn how to do things differently, like not argue over petty stuff, or play a fair basketball game and control my anger on the court. I also learned how to be patient by giving people at least three chances before I start to get mad. Once I got that down pat, my frustration lessened.

My staff and other people who knew me noticed the change. I felt good. Finally, I didn't feel like I had to bully kids. It felt kind of strange not being angry, but it wasn't something that I wanted back.

As I learned how to control my anger, I realized that I had things to look forward to in my life, like basketball, spades, and chess. So when I got mad I didn't stay stuck on my anger.

Now I feel I'm in a good place in my life. I still don't completely trust people. Most of the friends I've made are really acquaintances. But I made one close friend in my residential treatment center who is still my friend today. When I went home, it turned out he lived right next to me. We chill a lot and watch over each other. He's more like my brother than my friend.

I hang out with my family more and I feel closer to them than I did growing up. Now I just need to find me a nice woman who lives far away from me (in a nicer place) and chill. That's my solution to staying out of trouble.

"CAN I HOLLA ATCHA?"

by Allajah Young

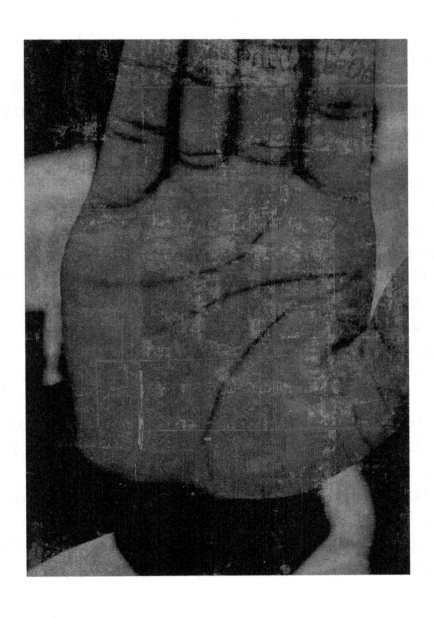

It's a hot, humid July day on Manhattan's Upper West Side, too hot to sit in the house. So my younger sister Ni and I venture out for frozen treats.

The trip across the street to the ice-cream cart isn't long, so I leave on my white tank top and put on a knee-length denim skirt and flip-flops. Too busy trying to decide whether I want cherry or mango, I fail to notice him leaning against a building next to the cart.

"Damn, Ma," he says.

What's that supposed to mean? Is that supposed to be a compliment? I instantly become unfriendly. He has the audacity to think I'm so simple. I roll my eyes as my face becomes rigid and mean.

"That boy's calling you, Allajah," says Ni, so innocently.

"Why does he have to say something?" I grunt to myself.

"Why you look so mean?" he says from under his oversized Yankees cap, which sits so low that I almost can't tell he's staring at me.

"Do you know him from your school?" Ni asks, puzzled.

"You know why I look so mean? Because I don't like you," I say to myself.

I am so weary of the idea that catcalls are an appropriate way to approach a girl on the street.

Catcalls can be tame, like "Pssss, pssss, where you live?" or outright dirty, like "Can you let me hit that?" It can be from one wanna-be-a-player guy on 125th Street in Harlem or from a group of delusional schoolboys on wealthy Madison Avenue.

Sometimes I can see it coming. I can see him looking at me lecherously from halfway down the block and no matter how much I look away, he can't hold back the comment that rolls off his tongue into my face.

"Damn, can I carry your bag?"

Or a dirty, raspy, "Hey sexy thang!"

And the common, "Can I holla atcha?"

But sometimes they come out of left field and take me by surprise, like the police officer who says, "God bless you, girl," as I pass him by. Street harassment's becoming more and more a part of my daily life. And the older I get, the more it exasperates me.

> **I feel uncomfortable when I'm gawked at or commented on. It's degrading. It's like I'm a car crash on the side of the highway, with men slowly rubbernecking their way past me so they can survey my every detail.**

Am I supposed to turn around and smile at you, delighted by your observation? Who are you looking for? The girl who turns around. The one whose standards aren't too high. The one who's sure to give you her number and go to your house the next day.

Those comments may work with those women, but not with me. I feel uncomfortable when I'm gawked at or commented on. It's degrading. It's like I'm a car crash on the side of the highway, with men slowly rubbernecking their way past me so they can survey my every detail. I simply don't respond, hoping they won't keep bothering me if I ignore them.

My boyfriend attributes the catcalls to the way most of my pants fit. Not that my pants are skin tight, but they are close. Still, even if my pants were painted on, does this give the dirty man in the corner store permission to stare directly at my behind as if I were the last piece of cake on the dessert cart?

Or if my top is cut low, does this give my teacher permission to stare directly down my shirt like he dropped something down there? Just like it's impolite to stare at the homeless or disabled, men shouldn't stare at a woman as if she's a movie poster.

Some men blame women for their harassment by saying that we dress provocatively and therefore want the stares and crass comments. But that argument has no merit, because unless a woman is walking down the street naked and screaming, "Come sleep with me!" what she wears is not necessarily an indication of what she wants sexually. Women wear tight pants and little shirts because we like them and they're common in stores.

And sometimes women try to outdress each other by wearing sexy outfits. A woman may want to be a sharp dresser in order to feel better about herself and feel attractive, not because she wants to be harassed by men.

Besides, we're still bothered even when we're not attractively dressed. When it's minus-2 degrees outside and I have on a pair of extra-large sweat pants, a huge bubble coat, and a fleece hat and scarf wrapped so tight on my head that only my eyes show, some simpleton will still say, "Yo. What up! Can I talk to you for a minute?"

I'm 17 and already feel like the harassment never ends. So I'm troubled when I see younger girls being harassed. I worry about Ni, who's only 11, and other girls her age because they're most susceptible to catcalls. They're often too young to see the lust and disrespect behind the comments and stares.

Sadly, I don't think I could stop the daily annoyances unless I shave my head or dress like a boy. But why should I have to? I'm not asking for much, just a little consideration.

I think some leftover animal instinct makes men stare, but that's no excuse for having no self-control. It's all right to glance at a woman you're attracted to, but to stare her down is unnecessary.

It's unfortunate that some girls and women welcome catcalls. This makes it harder for those of us with a certain level of self-respect. When I ignore the catcall games, I'm looked at like I'm the crazy one. But this doesn't faze me much because I don't want to be friends with someone who harasses women.

Sadly, I don't think I could stop the daily annoyances unless I shave my head or dress like a boy. But why should I have to? I'm not asking for much, just a little consideration.

So guys, if you're attracted to a girl you see on the street, approach her respectfully. Instead of jumping out from an alley and saying, "Yo pants is tiiiigggghhhht!!" try to approach her when she's waiting to cross the street.

Say, "Hello, how are you doing?" or "Excuse me, can I have a word with you?" Try to be calm and civilized. Remember, a vulgar comment will often completely reverse your chances of actually talking with the girl you're interested in.

Think about how you'd feel if the tables were turned and you had to deal with street harassment. I'm sure if, every day, you had to hear a big-bodied woman loudly proclaim to you how she wants to "hit that ass," you wouldn't be so quick to tell me the same. If you lived with that on a daily basis, you'd see why street harassment's so wearisome for women to cope with.

BAD BOY GETS A CONSCIENCE

by Anonymous

From the age of 10 to age 14, I was a monster. It was as if my conscience had taken a long vacation. I did horrible things to people and didn't care.

I ripped into other kids and mocked them till they cried. My friends and I called one kid "Bobby the Beaver" because of his teeth. We gnawed on pencils in front of him, making him squirm. And the other kids would laugh. We thought we were funny.

At school, I went into people's desks or bags and took their snacks or CDs. I stole from stores for the fun of it, too. I did it once and I got away with it, so that inspired me to do it again.

> **From the age of 10 to age 14, I was a monster. I did horrible things to people and didn't care. I never stopped to think why I did these things. I did them because I could.**

I enjoyed going into nice neighborhoods, like the Upper East Side of Manhattan, and scratching up expensive cars. I'd find a big gaudy car, like a Benz or a Lexus. Then I'd wait until no one was looking and scratch my initials on the trunk, and put "album coming soon."

I never stopped to think why I did these things. I did them because I could.

But now, a lot of people see me as Mr. Rogers, because I'm mostly friendly and unassuming. I do well in school. I'm helpful and polite. Most people assume that I've always been a good guy, but that's far from the case.

I think I got so mean because when I was younger, people in school picked on me. I had a bit of a stammer, and I was taller than most of the class. I was a very hyper but nice kid, but I got the vibe that people didn't like me and thought of me as stupid. We played charades once in class and though the correct word was "stupid," several kids called out my name as the answer. That hurt.

I had one close friend, but he left in fourth grade, and then I didn't have any friends. The other kids in school avoided me and the girls ran away from me in the yard. I felt alienated.

Since people didn't like me, I thought I might as well give them a reason. I started chasing the girls around and making monster noises. They hated it. But I thought it was funny.

Being picked on made me angry, and I started to fight back.

I wanted respect, and I discovered that if I acted tough, people respected me. Or maybe they feared me—I didn't understand the difference.

I turned being bigger to my advantage. My favorite activity was sitting on people. If someone said or did something to me, I'd push him on the floor and sit on him. "I could do this all day," I'd say. "I'm not getting off you until you apologize to me." I got my apologies.

I wanted respect, and I discovered that if I acted tough, people respected me. Or maybe they feared me—I didn't understand the difference. I fought over anything. I'd take on kids younger than me, my age, or older, whole groups, girls—anybody, as long as I thought I could win.

I liked the power I commanded over the situation and that made my actions bolder over time. I took things up a notch. A stare deserved a smart-ass comment, a smartass comment deserved a push, a push deserved a few punches, a few punches deserved getting stomped.

When I got to junior high school I was able to use my "talents" to acquire a group of like-minded friends. I was in charge. I admired my friends' humor, though. I'd point someone out and they would start dissing them.

I enjoyed being able to hurt people with words. We even harassed the teachers. One teacher quit after his first few months with us, and we went through five more until the school found

> **someone who could keep us more in check.**

I was particularly horrible to a kid named Billy. One time, I'd gotten a buzz-cut and he goofed on me. That annoyed me, so he became my pet project. For 10 months I did nothing but insult him. I'd get everybody to laugh at him in class or in the lunchroom. When we learned we were getting a snow day, I pointed to Billy and told him, "We'll get two days off if you stand on the roof and shake your head," because of his dandruff.

I enjoyed being able to hurt people with words. We even harassed the teachers. One teacher quit after his first few months with us, and we went through five more until the school found someone who could keep us more in check.

There was one teacher, though, who I respected. He was laid back and friendly, and he treated me like I could think and understand. He thought I was a smart kid and I took that to heart. He lent me a book about rap history and taught me to play chess.

And then there was Lisa. She was different from the other girls at my school. She was into art, books, classical music, and school—everything I wasn't. She was the first girl I fell in love with.

I think I was attracted to her because she acted so different and I wanted to know why. In my last year of junior high, I asked her to tutor me in math because it was the easiest way to start talking to her.

I acted really nice toward Lisa and we talked a lot during our tutoring sessions. Our conversations brought out my intellectual side. I was able to take the things I learned through my teacher and apply them to the conversations with Lisa. She expected me to understand things and that made me feel good. I came to really love her and enjoy her company.

But when Lisa caught on to how I felt about her, she totally crushed me. She sat me down one day and said, "I know that you like me."

"How did you know?" I asked.

She said she'd been reading *Seventeen* and there was a quiz, "Does one of your friends like you?"

"I took the test and it described you," she said. Then she said she could never see herself with me. "I think you're a horrible person," she said. "Get away from me."

It surprised me, because she was the first person I was ever really good to and I thought she at least liked me as a person. I was kind of numb for a while, and then I was in pain.

She stopped tutoring me and we stopped talking. And whenever her friends were around, she'd make a negative comment about me loud enough for me to hear it.

I almost never let anything faze me, but that did. I couldn't say anything back because I cared about her too much to hurt her. I felt the way I must've made people feel, small and hurt.

Around the same time, I had another experience that threw me off course. My friends and I were hanging out with some girls from school, and one girl was hanging on my friend Tommy. Suddenly, some high school guys ran up. They were a lot bigger than we were. The girl with Tommy was seeing one of them, and he walked up to Tommy, punched him and pushed him on the ground.

I ran. I left out of fear. I picked fights I could win, and I didn't think I could win this one. Some of my friends were mad at me. They questioned my loyalty. But I hated to lose a fight.

One of my friends really took it to heart and trashed me in school the next day. "You ran out on Tommy," he yelled at me.

"Well, you ran out, too," I shot back.

"I left to call the police. Where did you go?" he said.

We almost came to blows in front of everybody in the auditorium, but a teacher broke us up. The incident polarized my group of friends. While some supported me, I stopped hanging out with most of them.

These combined dramas took all the joy out of my work of being nasty. I got really depressed in the last couple of weeks of junior high school. I felt heartbroken by Lisa and bummed by what happened between my friends.

> **I started having nightmares where I'd be fighting what seemed like a marathon of people, until I couldn't fight anymore and was destroyed by the constant swarm of people coming at me. Looking back, it was fitting punishment for the way I'd treated people.**

My friends ended up going to a different high school from me, which only increased our distance. And when I started high school, I didn't know anyone. I got really reclusive and I sank into a depression. I didn't have my heart in harming people anymore. I tried it a few times, just to get my confidence going, but it didn't work.

I started having nightmares where I'd be fighting what seemed like a marathon of people, until I couldn't fight anymore and was destroyed by the constant swarm of people coming at me. Looking back, it was fitting punishment for the way I'd treated people.

In junior high I had so much power, but in high school I was nothing. I was anonymous and, more than anything, that drove me crazy. I wanted the same attention I got before, but I didn't want to harm people anymore. I didn't have guilt yet over what I did; I just didn't have the same sense of fun I used to have when I did something mean-spirited.

Without friends, I had nothing to do after school, so I'd read and write to pass the time. And because I was reading so much on my own, I started doing well in school. I could understand schoolwork much quicker than I had before.

But I had no meaningful contact with anyone for two years. I felt that I didn't know how to act toward people if they weren't in fear of me. I'd had few relationships that didn't revolve around my control of people. I became very brooding and quiet.

The closest I came to interacting with people was when I worked on the school newspaper, as editor. Most of the time I left comments on the writers' articles, rather than talk to them in person. Usually, after school or on weekends, I'd go to a bookstore or a library, or I'd go to the movies by myself.

But I became sick of feeling anonymous. I wanted a change. The first thing I did was change schools. I applied and got into an alternative school in the city.

My goal when I left my old high school was to learn how to be social and to interact normally with people my own age. I had to learn how to communicate my feelings and ideas without being mean or aggressive. I also had to learn to respect people and not to insist on what I wanted.

First, I started observing people. When I used to pick on people, I'd study them to see where they might be vulnerable. So I thought I should also study people I wanted to be my friends.

I'd watch people and the way they interacted. I made mental notes, like "This girl touches her friends as she talks to them; she's outgoing and seems well liked."

Then, I tried striking up conversations on the subway or bus, and in school. Sometimes people would open up to me, and I began to see people in a whole new light.

I began to see the beauty of people, something that never really struck me till I started to interact with them. I saw how frail a person can be, or how honest, or compassionate, or smart, or funny. I developed a sense of empathy. I started to understand what people are going through and have been through to act the way they do.

One person who helped set me on my current path was Anna. I met her on the bus. It was the first time I'd ever talked to a girl outside of school.

She had headphones on and I could hear the music, so I decided to ask her about it. I was nervous because she was beautiful, and my experience of interacting with pretty girls was that they usually looked down on me. When I introduced myself to her, I said my full name and she said, smiling, "I am Anna and the rest of my name I can't pronounce." She was funny and had a sarcasm that made her approachable.

I told her I was 16, and she said, "Aww, you're a baby." (She was 20, but looked younger.) If someone had said something like that to me before, I would've gotten upset, but the way she said it sounded like a compliment.

Anna was from Europe and would fall into an accent when she told stories about life in her country. We didn't spend much time together, but we'd talk on the phone once or twice a week. Then, for a week, I tried calling and couldn't reach her.

I liked learning about new people and trying to figure them out. I also felt that by trying to help people, I could make up for my past of harming people and being so indifferent to them.

When I did, she sounded sad. She told me her best friend had died and she was too depressed to do anything. It bothered me hearing her upset. But during our talk, I was able to make her laugh a few times and she told me that was the first time she'd laughed since her friend's death.

Making her feel better made me feel good. I was happy I could do that for her. Even though she moved away soon after that and we lost touch, my friendship with Anna made me realize how good it felt to help someone.

I got excited by my new concern. I liked learning about new people and trying to figure them out. I also felt that by trying to help people, I could make up for my past of harming people and being so indifferent to them.

I mainly talked to girls because they're generally more open to conversation. I was able to learn a lot about people because if I asked a girl what she was thinking or feeling, she'd usually tell me. Most guys would just say, "Nothing." But my best friend now is a guy, Otis, who I knew in my depressed stage. We developed a relationship as I built more confidence.

Now I enjoy connecting with people and I learn a lot about myself as I observe others. One day I decided to talk to Shelly, a girl in my class, because it seemed that no one else was paying attention to her. I thought she was smart, but she later told me that people talked down to her. I knew what that felt like.

She reminded me of myself. I know what it's like to be alone and I don't like thinking that other people are alone. Most people have their issues, but they're good at heart.

With Shelly, there's a high level of trust—I can tell her things and be vulnerable to her in the way that she can be vulnerable to me. She helps me feel better about things, too.

I don't expect a reward for how I've changed. Over time, I've learned that my goal shouldn't be to redeem myself, as if "poof!" what I did in the past can be erased. What makes me happy is relating to people, having them trust me, and letting them know that they're not all alone.

STANDING UP TO THE CYBERBULLIES

by Malik Frank, Breanna King, Angelica Sanchez, and Linda Sankat

Bullying has been around for a long, long time. But the relatively recent ability to harass, threaten, tease, and belittle people in front of a huge online audience has refocused public attention on this all-too-common crime.

According to the Cyberbullying Research Center, one in five teens has been a target of cyberbullying, which can range from teasing to death threats. Cyberbullying is often anonymous, so perpetrators can engage in it with little fear that they'll be held responsible.

> **One in five teens has been a target of cyberbullying, which can range from teasing to death threats.**

For some targets of cyberbullying, the vicious and very public ridicule has been too much. Some teens have even committed suicide in response to online harassment. It's gotten the public's attention. People have started blogs, Facebook pages, and Twitter accounts dedicated to raising awareness about how destructive bullying can be, and encouraging teens and adults alike to stand up against it.

Even the White House has gotten involved. President Barack Obama hosted a conference on bullying prevention, with the goal of destroying the "myth that bullying is just a harmless rite of passage or an inevitable part of growing up" instead of a vicious crime that can have devastating consequences for the target. Lady Gaga met with President Obama during a political fundraiser and urged him to continue addressing the bullying problem.

MAKING BULLYING LAWS TOUGHER

It's not just presidents and pop stars who are standing up to bullying, though. New York and New Jersey have taken a hard line against bullying, recognizing how hurtful—and dangerous—it can be. In September 2011, a New Jersey law took effect requiring school employees to identify and prevent harassment and bullying. Under the law, known as the Anti-Bullying Bill of Rights, schools must have a "school safety team" to respond to such incidents. If school administrators are caught not investigating bullying incidents, they can be disciplined.

When bullying happens in a public place like school, adults can more easily catch on and do something to stop the bullying (not that they always do). But cyberbullying is different. It happens online, where it's harder for adults to "overhear" what's going on.

Sometimes cyberbullying starts innocently, when someone gets bored and tries to play around without thinking about the effects on the other person. Other cyberbullying is intentionally mean, and it doesn't stop after the first time. When it happens, a lot of kids just keep their feelings inside and don't seek help, causing them to feel very hurt, and sometimes suicidal.

That's why New York State Senator Jeff Klein introduced a bill in 2011 that would treat online bullying of anyone under 21 as third-degree stalking, which is a misdemeanor. In cases where the cyberbullying leads to the target's suicide, however, the crime would become a felony with a possible 15-year prison sentence. The legislation was proposed in response to the suicide of Jamey Rodemeyer, a 14-year-old from western New York who was bullied for years about his sexuality, according to family members.

Rodemeyer took his life a year after Tyler Clementi, a freshman at Rutgers University, committed suicide by jumping off the George Washington Bridge. Clementi's suicide came after his roommate put a video on the Internet that showed Clementi having a sexual encounter with another man. That tragedy prompted U.S. Senator Frank Lautenberg and U.S. Representative Rush Holt, both of New Jersey, to introduce legislation in Congress to combat harassment and bullying on college campuses. The legislation would require all universities and colleges to have a harassment policy and to make students aware of resources, like mental health counseling and other services, to help targets and bullies alike.

Here's a look at some other ways people are saying, "No more."
—*With reporting by Malik Frank*

A THIN LINE

In early 2011, teen pop star Justin Bieber joined MTV, Facebook, Myspace, and a number of other organizations in taking a stand against cyberbullying by becoming a spokesperson for A Thin Line, MTV's campaign to fight online abuse. Bieber has spoken publicly about being the target of online jokes and abusive statements. The campaign is meant to get teens thinking about how a joke or comment may seem harmless but can easily spread online and end up devastating people's lives.

As part of the campaign, people have started blogs and anti-bullying groups to create more awareness about cyberbullying. MTV has created a way for people to have online conversations where they can talk about how bullying has affected their lives and discuss solutions.

Participating in A Thin Line is just one way that Facebook is addressing the problem. The company recently unveiled a new set of anti-bullying tools meant to create a culture of respect among its users. Why? The existence of Facebook has made it easy for this kind of bullying to happen. Most teens today have

Facebook pages, and Facebook is a place where cyberbullies like to hang out and do their dirty work.

> **The existence of Facebook has made it easy for this kind of bullying to happen. Facebook is a place where cyberbullies like to hang out and do their dirty work.**

In response, Facebook set up a Facebook Safety Center that offers several ways to report offensive or threatening content, all in one place. When you enter the safety center, you can use tools to block someone, control who sees your info, and report harassing messages. Facebook has also created places on users' pages to help them find answers to safety questions. These can be found under a Facebook user's privacy settings.

I investigated the "reporting harassing messages" tool. You can click the "report" link next to the sender's name on the message and remove the person as a friend. Reporting the message as harassment will also automatically block the person from communicating with you. Reports are confidential, so people you report don't automatically know they have been reported. After you submit a report, Facebook investigates the issue and determines the appropriate course of action.

—*Breanna King*

ONE PERSON CAN MAKE A DIFFERENCE

In the fall of 2011, Pennsylvania photographer Jennifer McKendrick had a senior portrait shoot scheduled with four girls. But before the photo shoot, McKendrick was on Facebook and came across a "burn page," which is a page created so students can write insulting comments about classmates for everyone to see.

According to the British newspaper the *Daily Mail,* McKendrick read the comments and was shocked by the vicious things some of the girls were saying. The perpetrators didn't talk about bad clothes or bad hair or ugly shoes; they talked about the target's sexuality. McKendrick recognized the names of the four girls posting the harassing comments. They were her clients—the ones who were scheduled for the upcoming senior portrait shoot.

McKendrick felt that she needed to intervene. She contacted the four girls' parents and told them she was canceling their shoot and returning their deposits. She explained to the parents what she'd seen, and shared a screen shot of the girls' comments as proof. The parents wrote her back and expressed their shock. They apologized for their children's behavior and informed McKendrick that they would speak with the girls.

According to the *Daily Mail,* McKendrick later wrote on her blog, "how could I spend two hours with someone during our session trying to make beautiful photos of them knowing they could do such ugly things?"

> **Many people get bullied mercilessly and have no one to be their voice. But McKendrick chose to help out a stranger who was being harassed online. If more people took the opportunity to speak out against cyberbullying like that, it might end.**

Dozens of people have written to McKendrick to applaud her for standing up to bullies. McKendrick said she knew refusing to photograph them wasn't going to make them better people or make them stop bullying others, but she didn't want people who act and say things like that to have any association with her business.

Even though McKendrick knew she couldn't stop bullying, she still got involved. It was courageous. Many people get bullied mercilessly and have no one to be their voice. But McKendrick chose to help out a stranger who was being harassed online. If more people took the opportunity to speak out against cyberbullying like that, it might end.

—Angelica Sanchez

USING CYBERSPACE TO STOP CYBERBULLYING

Sex advice columnist Dan Savage created the It Gets Better Project, in which he invited adults to share, via video, hopeful messages for lesbian, gay, bisexual, and transgender (LGBT) teens after several teens who'd been harassed and bullied about their sexuality committed suicide.

The project started with a single YouTube video. Dan and his partner Terry Miller posted a video encouraging LGBT teens to persevere despite adversity. "The worst time of life, really, for many gay kids is high school, and if at that time of your life you choose to end your life ... the bullies really won then, and you have deprived yourself of so much potential for happiness," they said.

> **"The worst time of life, really, for many gay kids is high school, and if at that time of your life you choose to end your life the bullies really won then, and you have deprived yourself of so much potential for happiness."**

Savage and Miller went on to describe the pain of their own childhoods. Savage had a strict Catholic upbringing, and he said "there were no gay people in my family and no openly gay people in my school and I was picked on 'cause ... I was obviously gay."

Miller also faced a great deal of harassment in school, never receiving the justice that he deserved. "My parents went in once to talk to the school administrators ... and they basically said 'If you look that way, walk that way, talk that way, act that way, then there's nothing we can do to help [you].'"

> **"My parents went in once to talk to the school administrators ... and they basically said 'If you look that way, walk that way, talk that way, act that way, then there's nothing we can do to help [you].'"**

The It Gets Better Project has received tens of thousands of video submissions. Each video features a person speaking a message of encouragement to LGBT teens. Entries have been submitted by people from all walks of life, gay and straight. A few notable entries include President Barack Obama, Secretary of State Hillary Clinton, Adam Lambert, Anne Hathaway, Colin Farrell, Matthew Morrison of *Glee,* Ellen DeGeneres, and people who work at a number of big corporations, including the Gap, Facebook, and Pixar.

Six months after it got started, the campaign released a book called *It Gets Better: Coming Out, Overcoming Bullying, and Creating a Life Worth Living.* The book had over 100 contributors, including religious leaders, politicians, parents, teachers, and teens. Savage's project spreads hope to the targets of all bullying, not just cyberbullying.

—*Linda Sankat*

Go to itgetsbetter.org to watch videos or to share your story.

TEENS TALK ABOUT ONLINE ABUSE

by YCteen *Staff*

If you read or watch much news, you've probably noticed that "cyberbullying" is a big topic these days. Media have extensively covered stories of teens and young adults driven to desperation and even suicide by taunts and aggression encountered online. Here, *YCteen*[1] summer writers discuss their own experiences and views of abuse and bad behavior online.

Describe examples of cyberbullying that you've heard of or encountered.

Neha Basnet: There's a Facebook page that basically has naked pictures of girls. The person who made it is anonymous, but if you have a revealing picture of a girl that you want posted on the website, you just send it to this person's email, and he or she posts it. Facebook has shut down the page, like, 20 times already, but whoever's making it keeps making backup pages.

I think Formspring, a site where people can ask each other questions anonymously, involves cyberbullying. People ask questions like, "Why are you so ugly?"

What do people get out of posting damaging pictures or negative comments about others?

Edward Francois: It's more emotional than logical. For one, it's a way to get revenge

---

[1] YCteen is a magazine written by New York City teens and published by Youth Communication.

because it's anonymous. The person is shamed and humiliated, and you get away with it scot-free.

Kiara Ventura: I think boys distribute naked pictures of girls because they just want to ruin the girls' reputations for whatever reason.

Edward: Or to show off: "This girl sent me a naked picture."

Neha: Maybe if you're jealous of someone. Or couples, when they break up, vent about each other just to get the other person mad.

Kiara: They're like, "Oh, I love being single!"

Neha: Yeah.

It sounds like people have an impulse to turn personal dramas into public ones.

Edward: Did anybody else do this when they were little: If you got angry at somebody, you'd write the most hurtful, evil thing you could say to a person—and then throw it in the garbage? That has prevented me from saying a lot of things to people. Putting it online is permanent. Putting it on paper and then throwing it away, burning it—that helps you get all your feelings out, and then just let it go. *Jozina Campbell:* But now that people have adapted to the Internet, they probably find it easier to go on their Facebook page than pick up a pen and paper.

Edward: The point of Facebook and similar websites is not to be private. It's whatever you're thinking, whatever you're feeling, whatever you wish you could do, just put it online.

"Going public" is only exciting if there's an audience. What makes you, as the audience, pay attention?

Kiara: I think it's because we're human—we're just nosy. It's like if you're on the highway and you see a car accident—obviously you'll look at it.

Why do humans want to see whatever awful thing is happening?

Jozina: Because everyone's going to be talking about it.

Kiara: Like in school, if there's a fight, people gather around whoever's fighting.

Neha: It's not something you see all the time. It's out of the ordinary, and it entertains you or amuses you.

Some of you have visited that page where the pictures of naked girls are posted. Do you find that site amusing?

Neha: No. Well, sometimes. I mean—if I see someone I don't know, I feel bad for them but it's like, "Why would you take a picture like that?" But when I did see someone I knew, that's when I felt really bad. Then it's personal.

How should a person react if they're being insulted or threatened online by a peer?

Jozina: People, no matter what, should defend themselves, so it doesn't look like whatever is being said about you is true. You can respond in a mature way; you don't have to bash the person who's attacking you.

Paldon Dolma: Telling your parents won't help, because they won't be with you 24-7. So I think it's better to defend yourself.

Edward: I used to be bullied, beaten up. I told my parents and they got involved, and I just got beat up even more.

But I think you have to tell somebody. Going it alone is not the best thing to do, because there could be more than one person doing this anonymously, and it's just you versus an unknown number.

Kiara: I think you should avoid the person, not even respond at all. You can easily block them on Facebook or AIM. If they post a picture of you, I don't know, untag yourself?

Edward: Don't take naked pictures of yourself, ever. And make sure the friends you have on Facebook are people you actually know in your life and talk to. Meeting a person one time doesn't mean they should be your friend on Facebook.

Paldon: Keep your Facebook profile private. You shouldn't write everything on Facebook.

Jozina: Watch the situations you get yourself into. Avoid talking to the wrong people in your school.

What do you think schools should do to prevent and combat cyberbullying?

Neha: In our school, the dean got involved when students were abusing Formspring. People were threatening others. Our school had a meeting where they told us, "Don't think you can do this anonymously anymore, because we can track you down if parents ask us to."

Schools have become more aware of cyberbullying, so now if you tell your parents and your parents tell the school, the school's able to arrange a meeting with the other person's parents—or even, if you want, they can look online and figure out who's doing it. At my school, when there's a problem, you sit down with the dean. You don't have to speak directly to the other person, but the dean will hear what you have to say. [The person doing the bullying] has to sign a paper that says he or she won't do anything like this anymore, kind of like a contract.

Edward: We've had assemblies saying that cyberbullying is wrong, but we've had assemblies about a lot of things—how to prevent pregnancy, how to prevent HIV, yet I see a girl in my school walking around carrying a baby. So it's good to get the message out, but you have to reinforce it. The teachers can't go online and just stop cyberbullying right there, but if it gets too serious, they should have a plan in place to put the brakes on somehow.

Neha, in your school, is there a punishment if the person bullying violates the contract?

Neha: I think you get suspended.

If you're a target of online abuse, should that be grounds for transferring schools?

Jozina: You should be able to transfer if it's really bad. Bullying can affect you in so many ways—kids are committing suicide over it. So I feel there should be action taken rather than the school just telling you, "Well, they didn't physically threaten you, they didn't physically do anything to you." So what? It's the same thing—it can get to that point where it's physical.

Neha: Especially because school is supposed to be a safe space, a learning space, and if you're not comfortable and you're distracted, it's going to keep you from your education.

Editor's Note: In June 2010, New York passed the Dignity for All Students Act to go into effect July 2012. This is a general anti-bullying measure that does not specifically address cyberbullying, but it requires school districts to "create policies and guidelines" to keep schools free from harassment, to help employees recognize and respond to harassment when it occurs, and to train at least one staff member in anti-discrimination counseling, among other things.

For more details, see: nysenate.gov/press-release/dignity-all-students-act.

VICIOUS CYCLES

by Miguel Ayala

Growing up, I felt so alone in this world. I never had any friends and I was bullied by just about everyone. My mom abused me at home and I think that kept me from making friends in school. I was afraid of rejection and afraid that my classmates would turn violent toward me.

> **Kids at school really would pick on me. I would think, "Why me? Why won't they leave me alone?"**

Kids at school really would pick on me. I used to wear no-frills clothing, and they would say that I was poor and I got my clothing from the Salvation Army. I would think, "Why me? Why won't they leave me alone?"

Soon I started to be the bully. I started picking on others who were smaller and weaker than I was. I was pissed off and I wanted to see how it felt to pick on someone. I would say, "Hey dweeb!" or "Wassup shrimp?" Sometimes I would push the kid. In the short run I felt good because, being the tormentor, I got a glimpse at power. But in the long run I didn't feel much better. I knew I didn't want to do to other people what my mom did to me.

Living with violence at home and abuse at school, I grew deeply depressed. I stayed to myself and one time I tried to end my life. Eventually I was removed from my mother's home and put in a group home. That's when I found out that bullying happens in foster care, too. In fact, in all the group homes I've been in, it's been a serious problem, one that isn't taken seriously enough.

In group homes, I've been bullied about my sexuality, my weight, and the fact that I take medication. Kids have called me names, hit me, and put mustard, ketchup, and dish detergent on my bed linens. I have also witnessed other kids who live with me get bullied in the same way. One resident got snuffed in the face for saying something stupid. That was so painful for me to see. It made me feel like my mom was hitting me. All the staff did was say, "Don't do that."

Why are group homes full of bullies? I went to Jonathan Cohen, a therapist and the cofounder and president of the National School Climate Center (formerly the Center for Social and Emotional Education) in New York City, to answer that question. Cohen said that bullying is a form of abuse, and that too many people assume that it's harmless and normal behavior for kids, when it is actually very harmful.

Cohen said that many kids who are abused or bullied tend to become bullies themselves. He said that people who are being abused feel small and helpless and ashamed. They might feel like the abuse is their fault. Hurting someone else may make them feel a little less helpless for a while.

> **"Bullying someone smaller than us or someone who has a disadvantage or who is different can make someone feel more powerful in the short run."**

"No one likes to feel helpless," explained Cohen. "Bullying someone smaller than us or someone who has a disadvantage or who is different can make someone feel more powerful in the short run."

Most kids in group homes have been abused or neglected. As children, many of us were made to feel small and helpless, often by our parents. So it makes sense that a lot of kids in group homes bully. By hurting others, they're trying to feel better about themselves.

Also, some people who have grown up with abuse think abuse is a form of caring. "Repeated, serious abuse can cause a person to develop the upside-down idea that being close to someone else is the same as being bullied by someone else," said Cohen. "It can make you feel like it's normal to be bullied." People who have been abused in the past are more likely to be targets today, he said.

> **Many teens who have been abused by their parents or someone else they care about have come to believe that bullying and abuse is a normal way to show love.**

I was abused by my mom for years. I knew I didn't like being victimized by her, but I also thought it was normal. I began to accept my mother's abuse as a form of love from her. When she hit me, later she would say, "I'm sorry. I have been through so much and I just wasn't thinking straight. Please forgive me." And you know what? I did forgive her. Over and over again.

Like me, many teens who have been abused by their parents or someone else they care about have come to believe that bullying and abuse is a normal way to show love. This may make them feel like hurting the people they love, or it may make them accept abuse from someone they are close to.

Also, when someone hasn't received much attention in her lifetime—like when someone is neglected by her parents—she might feel that bullying is okay because it's a form of attention. She may think, "At least the person who's bullying me is acknowledging my presence." Targets of abuse may go as far as to seek out people who are likely to bully them.

> **Bullying is not a good way to feel bigger and better than someone. Nor is it a way to show or receive love from someone. Bullying is not love.**

But bullying is not a good way to feel bigger and better than someone. Nor is it a way to show or receive love from someone. Bullying is not love. It can have serious consequences, like depression, for both the target and the person bullying.

"Ongoing bullying can and does make someone feel helpless and that can lead to serious depression," said Cohen. Research has also shown that children who bully other children are at risk for more violent behavior. That's why it's so important that adults pay attention to bullying and help stop it.

But too often, said Cohen, adults do not intervene when they see or hear bullying. That happens in group homes a lot. Cohen said that if adults just sit aside and do nothing about bullying, they risk putting a child in harm's way and they risk sending the message that bullying is okay. But bullying is not okay. "Bullying is emotionally and socially toxic," said Cohen.

When a person in a group home who bullies isn't stopped, everyone in that group home lives in fear. Especially for kids who have been removed from their homes due to abuse, living in fear of bullying is no way to live.

HOW ADULTS CAN HELP

by Miguel Ayala

Research has shown that adults can significantly change the pattern of bullying. Giving consequences for bullying or stopping a problem before it escalates can and will make a difference, said therapist Jonathan Cohen, cofounder and president of National School Climate Center in New York City. Here's what Cohen said adults can do to help stop bullying:

1. Get help for the person who is bullying. Send the child who is bullying into some sort of psychotherapy, because this type of abuse can really mess up the head of the child bullying (and of the target). Without therapy, a person might not be able to grow out of bullying. Research has shown that bullying can lead to more violent behavior.

2. Teach the person who is bullying. Teach the kid bullying how to pay attention to what he or she is feeling. Sometimes when a person bullies, it is because he feels overwhelmed at the moment and doesn't know what he's feeling. If he can understand his feelings better, he can figure out what's bothering him and maybe even talk about it without taking it out on someone else.

3. Intervene. If there's a conflict, sit down with the person bullying and the target and talk about the problem. Separate individuals who are arguing and try to settle the problem. If the teens live together (like in a group home), set up a system where every single day the house members will sit down and have a meeting.

Bullying is not normal behavior, and it can do great harm to both the person who bullies and the targets. Research shows that even witnesses of bullying can be hurt psychologically. But when adults intervene, they can help change the pattern of bullying. Research has proven that! Adults—especially staff at group homes where bullying is far too common—need to stop sitting by when bullying happens. They need to stand up and make a difference. Help us break the pattern of bullying and being bullied that runs in many of our lives.

ABOUT YOUTH COMMUNICATION

Youth Communication, founded in 1980, is a nonprofit educational publishing company located in New York City. Its mission is to help marginalized teens develop their full potential through reading and writing, so that they can succeed in school and at work and contribute to their communities.

Youth Communication publishes true stories by teens that are developed in a rigorous writing program. It offers more than 50 books that adults can use to engage reluctant teen readers on an array of topics including peer pressure, school, sex, and relationships. The stories also appear in two award-winning magazines, *YCteen* and *Represent,* and on the website (www.youthcomm.org), and are frequently reprinted in popular and professional magazines and textbooks. Youth Communication offers hundreds of lessons, complete leader's guides, and professional development to guide educators in using the stories to help teens improve their academic, social, and emotional skills.

Youth Communication's stories, written by a diverse group of teen writers, are uniquely compelling to peers who do not see their experiences reflected in mainstream reading materials. They motivate teens to read and write, encourage good values, and show teens how to make positive changes in their lives.

You can access many of the stories and sample lessons for free at www.youthcomm.org. For more information on Youth Communication's products and services, contact Loretta Chan at 212-279-0708, x115, or lchan @youthcomm.org.

Youth Communication
224 West 29th Street, 2nd Floor
New York, NY 10001
212-279-0708
www.youthcomm.org

ABOUT THE EDITOR

Hope Vanderberg was the editor of *New Youth Connections* (now called *YCteen),* Youth Communication's magazine by and for New York City teens, from 2004 to 2008.

Prior to working at Youth Communication, Hope specialized in science journalism and environmental education. She was an editor at Medscape.com, a medical website, wrote articles for *Audubon* and *The Sciences* magazines, and taught children and teens at environmental education centers in California and Texas. She has also worked as a field biologist, studying bird behavior in Puerto Rico.

She has a master's degree in science and environmental journalism from New York University and a bachelor's degree from Earlham College. She is currently a freelance editor.

Real Teen Voices Series

Pressure

True Stories by Teens About Stress
edited by Al Desetta of Youth Communication

Stress hits these teen writers from all angles; they're feeling the pressure at school, at home, and in their relationships. The young writers describe their stress-relief techniques, including exercise, music, writing, and more. The collection includes tips for cooling down and inspiring examples of perseverance. For ages 13 & up.

Rage

True Stories by Teens About Anger
edited by Laura Longhine of Youth Communication

The teen writers in *Rage* have plenty of reasons to be angry: parental abuse, street violence, peer pressure, feeling powerless, and more. The writers give honest advice and talk about their anger management skills as they struggle to gain control of their emotions and stop hurting others—and themselves. For ages 13 & up.

Vicious

True Stories by Teens About Bullying
edited by Hope Vanderberg of Youth Communication

Essays by teens address bullying: physical, verbal, relational, and cyber. These stories will appeal to readers because the cruelty and hurt are unmistakably real—and the reactions of the writers are sometimes cringe-worthy, often admirable, and always believable. For ages 13 & up.

Interested in purchasing multiple quantities and receiving volume discounts? Contact edsales@freespirit.com or call 1.800.735.7323 and ask for Education Sales. **Many Free Spirit authors are available for speaking engagements, workshops, and keynotes.** Contact speakers@freespirit.com or call 1.800.735.7323.

For pricing information, to place an order, or to request a free catalog, contact:

**Free Spirit Publishing Inc.
217 Fifth Avenue North • Suite 200 • Minneapolis, MN 55401-1299
toll-free 800.735.7323 • local 612.338.2068
• fax 612.337.5050**

help4kids@freespirit.com ● www.freespirit.com

BACK COVER MATERIAL

VICIOUS

True Stories by Teens About Bullying

Kiara and her friends are terrorized by a cyberbully.

Jeremiyah is constantly attacked because he is gay.

Elie fights back so hard against bullies he becomes a bully himself—and loses friends.

In *Vicious,* teen writers tell about their experiences with bullying of all kinds: physical, verbal, relational, and cyber. The cruelty and hurt they experience are unmistakably real, and so are their struggles to protect themselves and their friends.

Whether they were bullied, bullied others, or witnessed bullying, these writers' stories are at times painful, often admirable, and always compelling for the resilience they reveal.

Lightning Source UK Ltd.
Milton Keynes UK
UKOW07f2205300616

277364UK00001B/22/P